***EYES ONLY*

MW01284994

Senior Executive Intelligence Brief

The SEIB must be returned to CIA within 5 working days

National Security Information

Unauthorized Disclosure Subject to Criminal Sanctions

APPROVED FOR RELEASE
DATE: MAR 2004

First Earth Battalion
NEW EARTH ARMY

****** EYES ONLY ******

~~Top Secret~~

PASS SEIB 99-090CX

What is a Warrior Monk?

Lt. Colonel Jim Channon
author, *1st EBN Field Manual*

"I envision an international ideal of service in an awakening class of people who are best called revolutionaries. I see them as soldiers, as youth, and as those who have soldier-spirit within them. I see them come together in the name of people and planet to create a new environment of support for the positive growth of humankind and the living earth mother.

Their mission is to protect the possible and nurture the potential. They are evolutionary guardians who focus their loving protection and affirm their allegiance to people and planet for their own good and for the good of those they serve. I call them evolutionaries, not revolutionaries, for they are potentialists, not pragmatists. They are pioneers, not palace guards.

As their contribution to a hopeful future, the warrior monks bring evolutionary tactics. They recognize that the world community of peoples demands hope from those who operate as servants to the people. Services rendered by the warriors of the First Earth Battalion are specifically designed to generate workable solutions to defuse regional and national conflicts, promote international relations, spread wise energy use, enforce the ecological balance, assist wise technological expansion, and above all, stress human development.

This will not be the first time that warrior monks have been active. In Vedic traditions, the warrior monk was a philosopher and a teacher, and therefore a powerful transformational player. In the Chinese culture, the warrior was both a healer and teacher of martial arts. History affirms our own belief that there is no contradiction in the warrior and the service-oriented monk prototypes living completely harmonious, blended and paralleled path when the bass ethic and service is 'loving protection' of evolution and humankind. There is no contradiction in having armies of the world experience the same ethic as they evolve in peaceful cooperation towards the greater good of all.

Armies are both the potential instruments of our destruction and the organized service that can drive humanity's potential development. They are the "turn-key" organization that can either shift the energy of our world into a positive synergistic convergence, or bring us to the brink of destruction. We have no choice but to encourage world armies to accept and express the nobility they already strive to attain. I can see their action expanding to include evolutionary work like planting vast new forests, completing large canal projects, and helping in the design and construction of new energy-solvent towns.

Military members and citizens can work together to clean up the inner cities, and working with the troubled inner city youth in young commando groups. I envision our nation working harmoniously with other nations to see that the plentiful resources of our mother earth are equally shared by all peoples."

-author, Lt. Col. Jim Channon, *Commander of the New Earth Army*

This edition compiled by www.YouthProject.US

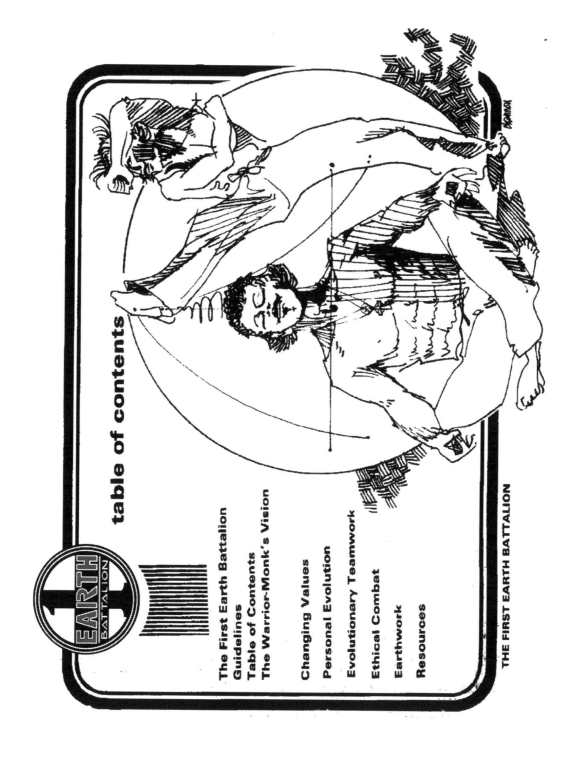

table of contents

The First Earth Battalion
Guidelines
Table of Contents
The Warrior-Monk's Vision

Changing Values
Personal Evolution
Evolutionary Teamwork
Ethical Combat
Earthwork
Resources

THE FIRST EARTH BATTALION

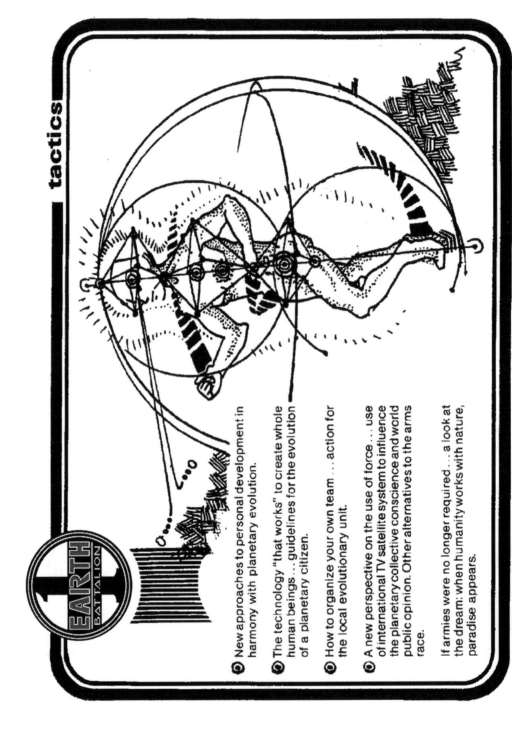

① New approaches to personal development in harmony with planetary evolution.

② The technology "that works" to create whole human beings... guidelines for the evolution of a planetary citizen.

③ How to organize your own team... action for the local evolutionary unit.

④ A new perspective on the use of force... use of international TV satellite system to influence the planetary collective conscience and world public opinion. Other alternatives to the arms race.

If armies were no longer required... a look at the dream: when humanity works with nature, paradise appears.

THE FIRST EARTH BATTALION

the warrior monk's vision
by Lt. Col Jim Channon, US Army

I envision an international ideal of service awakening in an emerging class of people who are best called *evolutionaries*. I see them as soldiers, as youth, and as those who have soldier spirit within them. I see them come together in the name of *people* and *planet* to create a new environment of support for the positive growth of humankind and the living earth mother. Their mission is to protect the possible and nurture the potential. They are the evolutionary guardians who focus their loving protection and affirm their allegiance to people and planet for their own good and for the good of those they serve. I call them evolutionaries, not revolutionaries, for they are potentialists, not pragmatists. They are pioneers, not palace guards.

As their contribution to a hopeful future, the warrior monks bring evolutionary tactics. They recognize that the world community of peoples demands hope from those who would operate as servants of the people. Services rendered by the warriors of the First Earth Battalion are specifically designed to generate workable solutions to defuse the nuclear time bomb, promote international relations, spread wise energy use, enforce the ecological balance, assist wise technological expansion, and above all, stress human development.

Armies are both the potential instruments of our destruction and the organized service that can drive humanity's potential development. They are the 'turn key' organizations that could either shift the energy of our world into a positive synergistic convergence, or bring us to the brink of the void. We have no choice but to encourage world armies to accept and express the nobility they already strive to attain. I can see their action expanding to include evolutionary work like planting vast new forests, completing large canal projects, helping in the design and construction of new energy-solvent towns, helping to clean up the inner cities, and working with the troubled inner city youth in young commando groups, and working harmoniously with other nations to see that the plentiful resources of our mother earth are equally shared by all peoples.

This will not be the first time that warrior monks have been active. In Vedic traditions, the warrior monk was a philosopher and teacher, and therefore a powerful transformational player. In the Chinese culture, the warrior was both a healer and teacher of martial arts. History affirms our own belief that there is no contradiction in the warrior and the service oriented monk prototypes living a completely harmonious, blended and parallel path when the basic ethic and service is 'loving protection' of evolution and humankind. There is no contradiction in having armies of the world experience the same ethic as they evolve in peaceful co-operation towards the greater good of all.

THE FIRST EARTH BATTALION

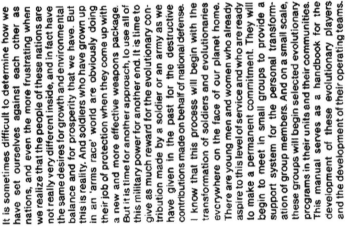

It is sometimes difficult to determine how we have set ourselves against each other as nations, and even the more frustrating when we realize that the people of these nations are not really very different inside, and in fact have the same desires for growth and environmental balance and for prosperity that we have. But this is reality. And soldiers who have grown up in an 'arms race' world are obviously doing their job of protection when they come up with a new and more effective weapons package. But it is time for another approach, to use all of this military power for another end. It is time to give as much reward for the evolutionary contribution made by a soldier or an army as we have given in the past for the destructive contributions made on behalf of national defense.

I know that this process will begin with the transformation of soldiers and evolutionaries everywhere on the face of our planet home. There are young men and women who already aspire to this level of service and who are ready to make a permanent commitment. They will begin to meet in small groups to provide a support system for the personal transformation of group members. And on a small scale, these groups will begin selected evolutionary programs in their units and their communities. This manual serves as a handbook for the development of these evolutionary players and the development of their operating teams.

All national level armies will begin to cooperate on ventures that stabilize the nuclear balance of terror. Joint teams could then patrol space

I welcome you to share in the Warrior Monk's vision, and also to share in helping it become a reality. We have no seriously satisfying alternative but to be wonderful.

and counter local terrorist activities that threaten stability in any given areas. Evolved cooperation will stifle the arms race. Cooperation between the Soviets and American military could insure that neither side "flies off the handle" in direct collision in some local arena of tension, which would precipitate both sides into a major nuclear war. And there are precedents for this type of cooperation unknown to the public. The US and Soviet military have partied together in Potsdam. They have exchanged academics at the Staff College level, and they have viewed each other's military exercises in recent years.

The great flow of historical events, habits, and international relations is not easy to change. It will take the patient, focused, loving and dedicated effort of warriors all over the world, people of different languages and cultures and all examples of humanity's infinite variety of expression. What I present in this manual is a small contribution to what surely must be a hope for peace and prosperity that lives in all hearts everywhere. It is not a set system of beliefs and ideas. It is a smorgasbord of new functional ideas. As you respond to these insights, you will be able to adjust them to your own operating style. They should flow into your culture and respond to your country's point of view. Any elaboration on these ideas can then come from your own study. They must work for everyone in some way or they won't really work.

THE FIRST EARTH BATTALION

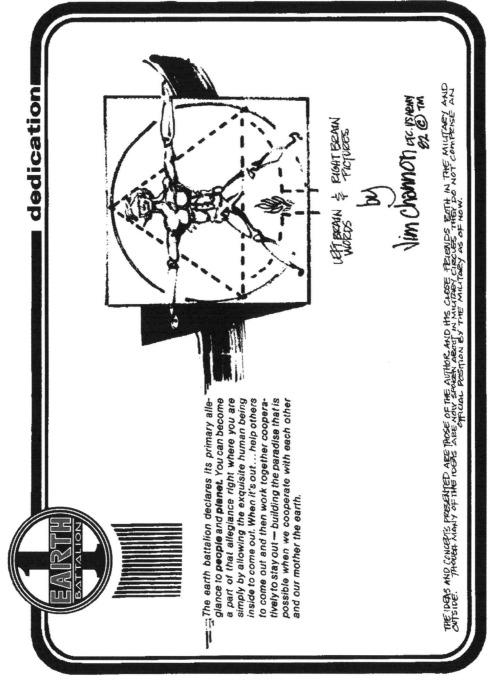

The earth battalion declares its primary allegiance to **people** and **planet.** You can become a part of that allegiance right where you are simply by allowing the exquisite human being inside to come out. When it's out... help others to come out and then work together cooperatively to stay out — building the paradise that is possible when we cooperate with each other and our mother the earth.

LEFT BRAIN & RIGHT BRAIN WORDS & PICTURES

by

Jim Channon LTC. USARM 82 © ™

THE IDEAS AND CONCEPTS PRESENTED ARE THOSE OF THE AUTHOR AND HIS CLOSE FRIENDS BOTH IN THE MILITARY AND OUTSIDE. THOUGH MANY OF THE IDEAS ARE NOW SPOKEN ABOUT IN MILITARY CIRCLES THEY DO NOT COMPRISE AN OFFICIAL POSITION BY THE MILITARY AS OF NOW.

THE FIRST EARTH BATTALION

THE FIRST EARTH BATTALION

The First Earth Battalion is a banner under which the forces of good in the world can unite and find strength in spirit with others who share a common goal. Warrior Monks are guardians of the good, guardians of humanity, nature and the planet. Warrior Monks in the United States Army are already teaching soft tactics. Others in the fields of economics, politics, and international affairs are already searching for new ways to work for the greater good in their own arenas. The modern Citizen Samurai in day to day existence is engaged in moral combat to reorganize and focus personal life to its highest good.

This manual was created from the ideas and teachings of over a hundred groups on the New Age Frontier of the West Coast of the United States. It is a primary tool to assist you in giving and getting the most possible from your experience in a human form in the physical realm of this planet earth. It will assist you in preparing for possibilities and events about which you may presently not even be able to dream. Prepare yourself so you will be ready, . . . Begin your work locally until the call goes out for global action.

guidelines

The manual is a self instructional workbook which contains operational procedures for changing old patterns of action into new ones. The reader can benefit by practicing the exercises contained and by reading and studying the manual as a reference textbook.

Awareness training, bodywork, martial arts, and spirit work are included in the manual as well as the advanced tactical ideas of the First Earth Battalion itself. Visual concepts will help the reader grasp many of the multi-dimensional ideas. A bibliography is included for further study. Where possible, names and addresses of various groups are included for the training described.

The ideas included are the most powerful and workable concepts gleaned from visits to over one hundred advanced advanced human performance useful for many to do the work in some detail and then periodically use the pages as "flash cards" to keep their awareness at the highest useful level.

This manual is experimental and will be revised after the first limited edition goes out . . . is critiqued . . . added to . . . and refined for mass consumption. The drawings and verbiage were executed by Jim Channon after each of his visits. The follow-up manuals or supplements promise to continue these reports from the frontier of the third wave world.

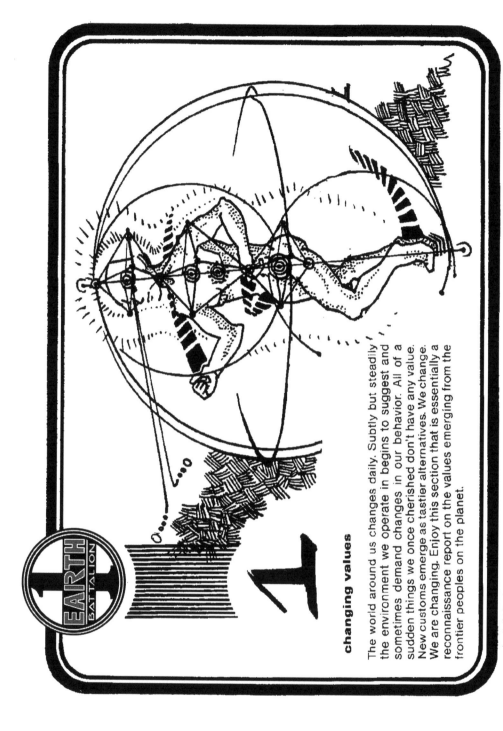

changing values

The world around us changes daily. Subtly but steadily the environment we operate in begins to suggest and sometimes demand changes in our behavior. All of a sudden things we once cherished don't have any value. New customs emerge as tastier alternatives. We change. We are changing. Enjoy this section that is essentially a reconnaissance report on the values emerging from the frontier peoples on the planet.

THE FIRST EARTH BATTALION

those who strive after the truth and
travel extensively in their quest are
known as warriors. they are
capable ... they get the job done.
good soldiers are also known as
warriors.   THE FIRST EARTH
wants the action orientation of
the warrior ... but tempered with
the patience and sensitivity and
ethics of the monk.   these are
the soldiers who have the power
to make paradise.   Why go
for anything less.

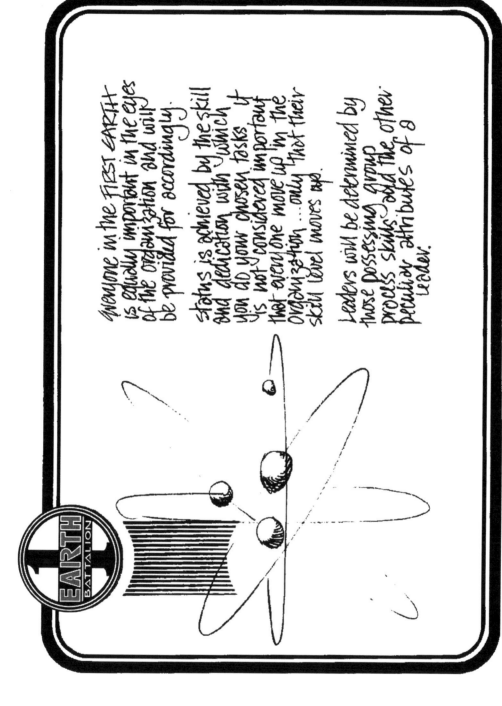

Everyone in the FIRST EARTH is equally important in the eyes of the organization and will be provided for accordingly.

Status is achieved by the skill and dedication with which you do your chosen tasks. It is not considered important that everyone move up in the organization... only that their skill level moves up.

Leaders will be determined by those possessing group process skills and the other peculiar attributes of a leader.

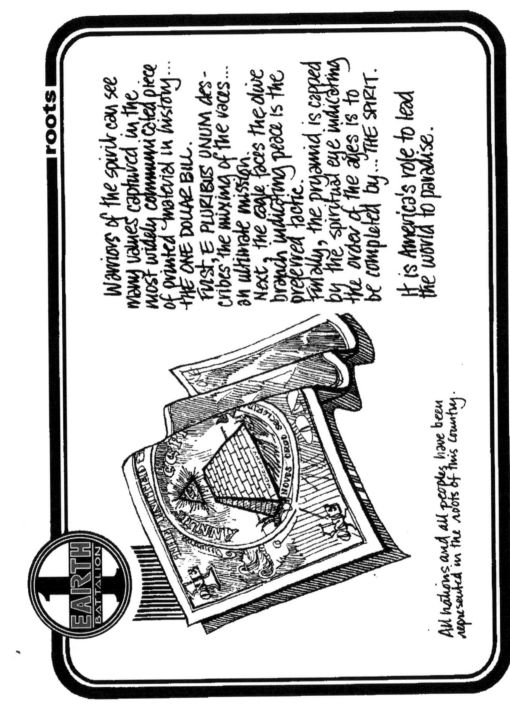

Warriors of the spirit can see many values captured in the most widely communicated piece of printed material in history... THE ONE DOLLAR BILL.

First, E PLURIBUS UNUM describes the mixing of the voices... an ultimate mission.

Next, the eagle faces the olive branch indicating peace is the preferred tactic.

Finally, the pyramid is capped by the spiritual eye indicating the order of the ages is to be completed by... THE SPIRIT.

It is America's role to lead the world to paradise.

All nations and all peoples have been represented in the roots of this country.

THE FIRST EARTH BATTALION

10

missions
EARTH BATTALION
thinkers in the third wave know that collecting solutions just increases your options.
WORLD LEADERS NEED MORE OPTIONS!
The president needs a wider range of solutions to deal with the 1980's. Force as an option has lost much of its flexibility. We need increased creativity.
FIRST EARTH BATTALION
ECO PIONEERS
SPACE PIONEERS
HUMAN DISASTER RESCUE GROUP
URBAN PIONEERS
ECO DISASTER RESCUE GROUP
NATURAL DISASTER RESCUE GROUP
FORCE OF HEART
FORCE OF WILL
FORCE OF ARMS
FORCE OF SPIRIT
SENSING
THE STAR
PEOPLE
SIGNALS
DESIGN
SUPPORT
EARTH
STAR
ARMS
HEART
WILL
SPIRIT
SPACE PIONEERS
ECO PIONEERS
URBAN PIONEERS
NATURAL DISASTER
ECO DISASTER
HUMAN DISASTER
counter-force company
pioneer company
rescue company

THE FIRST EARTH BATTALION

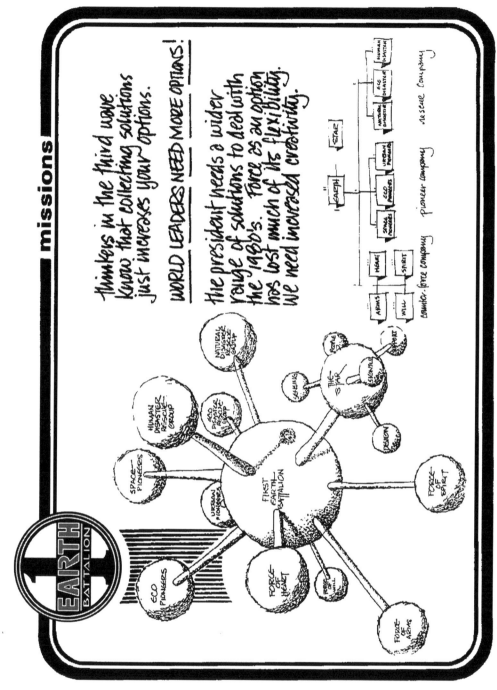

can you trace the values shift in the military?

THE FIRST EARTH BATTALION

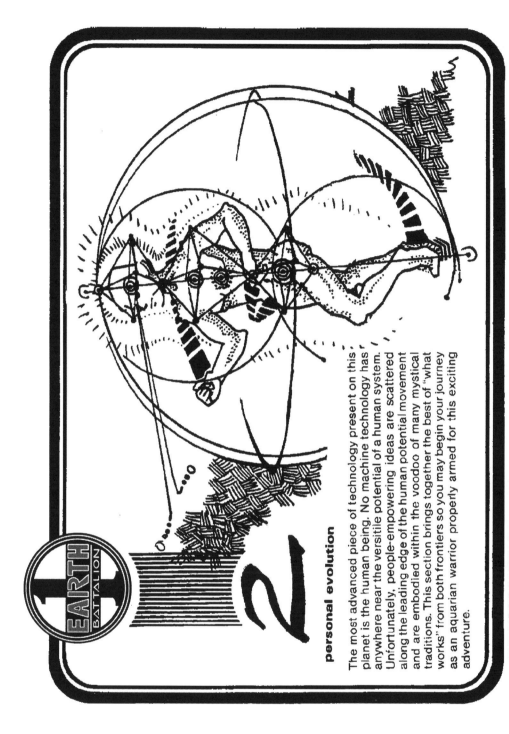

personal evolution

The most advanced piece of technology present on this planet is the human being. No machine technology has anywhere near the versitile potential of a human system. Unfortunately, people-empowering ideas are scattered along the leading edge of the human potential movement and are embodied within the voodoo of many mystical traditions. This section brings together the best of "what works" from both frontiers so you may begin your journey as an aquarian warrior properly armed for this exciting adventure.

personal evolution

The universe is perfect just as it is. It gives you,the individual, just what you need and no more. In this way you can experience a progressively more interesting life from moment to moment. When you cooperate with the universe, it makes this trip into an expanded awareness; a smooth and delicious experience. When you ignore the evolutionary masterplan, the universe will expand your awareness just the same, but the trip is then bumpy and often very painful. In this section of the manual you will be given insight into some time honored and also some new technology needed to make your personal adventure in this world both creative and enjoyable.

The manual focuses on key evolutionary actions that you can master. These actions can create positive visions for you that will change your life the very moment you begin practicing them. These actions will enable you to steer your awareness and therfore evaluate your experience through what have been heretofore boring or painful moments.

There are many ways to experience each moment. Some people seem to enjoy them all. Some masters can experience many of them in various states of ecstacy. But we know\or most people, life has its ups and downs, and then there are some people who manage not to enjoy any of it at all.

Gaining leverage over the life experience can come through a key set of lessons for both success and enlightenment. Fortunately, the best schools on the subject moved to the United States in recent years and were available for our research. The following key technology has been selected from the works of over a hundred schools both orthodox and mystical, traditional and futuristic, and specially oriented on the paths of both personal and planetary evolution. These tools will work for you to the extent that you use them. That's a promise.

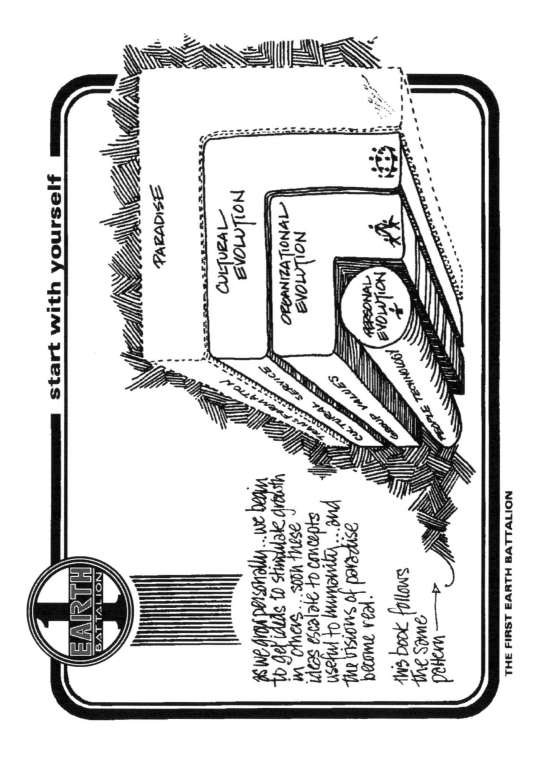

start with yourself

PARADISE

CULTURAL EVOLUTION

ORGANIZATIONAL EVOLUTION

PERSONAL EVOLUTION

CULTURAL SERVICE

GROUP VALUES

PEOPLE TECHNOLOGY

As we grow personally... we begin to get ideas to stimulate growth in others... soon these ideas escalate to concepts useful to humanity... and the visions of paradise become real.

This book follows the same pattern ➝

THE FIRST EARTH BATTALION

15

the path of personal evolution

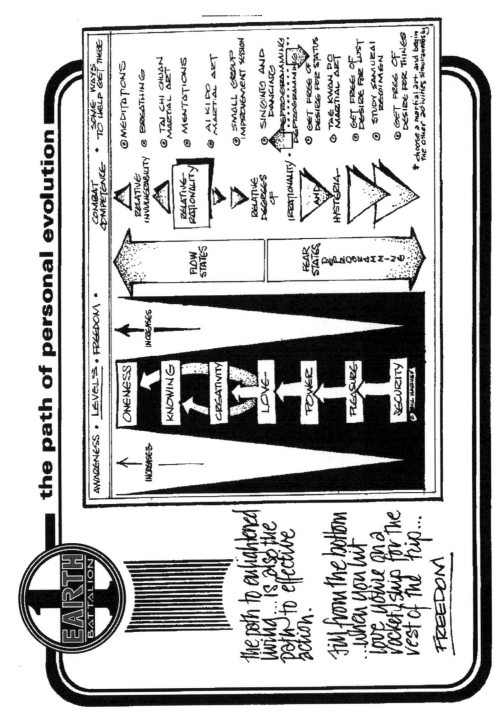

THE FIRST EARTH BATTALION

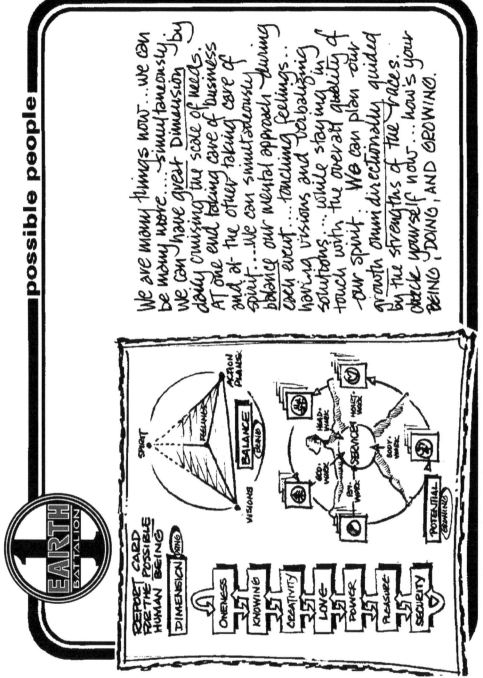

We are many things now ... we can be many more ... simultaneously, we can have great Dimension by daily cruising the scale of needs. At one end taking care of business and at the other taking care of spirit ... we can simultaneously balance our mental approach during each event ... touching feelings ... having visions and verbalizing solutions ... while staying in touch with the overall quality of our spirit. We can plan our growth omnidirectionally guided by the strengths of the faces. Check yourself now ... how's your BEING, DOING, AND GROWING.

THE FIRST EARTH BATTALION

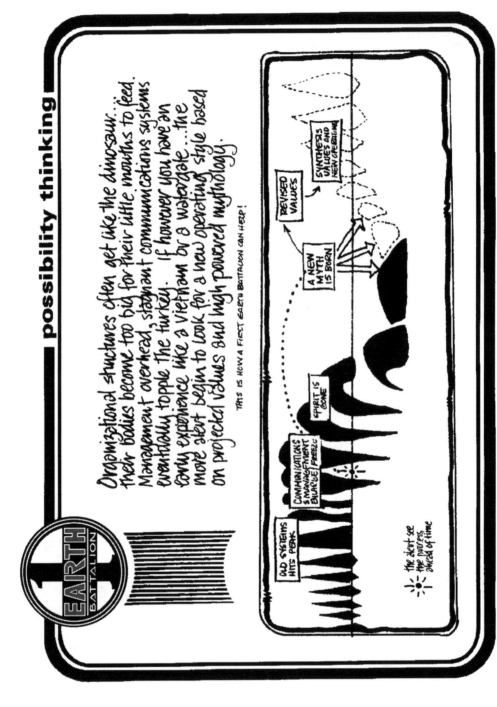

Organizational structures often get like the dinosaur... their bodies become too big for their little mouths to feed. Management overhead, stagnant communications systems eventually topple the turkey. If however you have an corny experience like a vietnam or a watergate ...the more alert begin to look for a new operating style based on projected values and high powered mythology.

THIS IS HOW A FIRST EARTH BATTALION CAN HELP!

OLD SYSTEMS HITS PEAK

COMMUNICATIONS & MANAGEMENT BALANCE FREEZE

SPIRIT IS GONE

A NEW MYTH IS BORN

REVISED VALUES

SYNTHESIS VALUES AND NEW OPERATING

the skout see the phases ahead of time

THE FIRST EARTH BATTALION

18

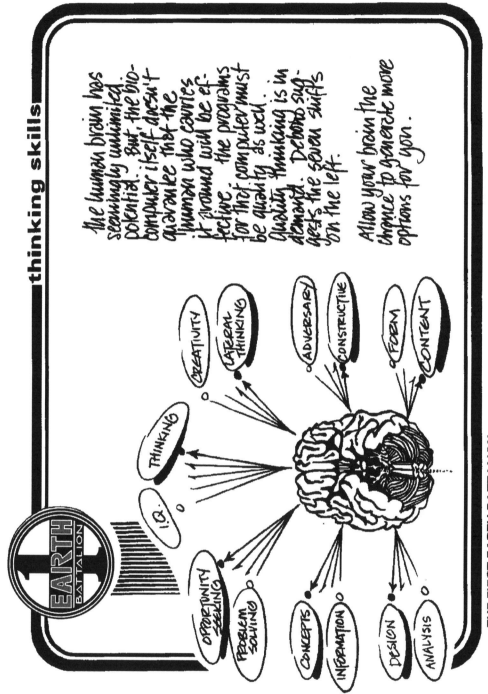

The human brain has seemingly unlimited potential. But, the bio-computer itself doesn't guarantee that the human who carries it around will be effective. the programs for that computer must be quality as well. Quality thinking is in demand. DeBono suggests the seven skills on the left.

Allow your brain the chance to generate more options for you.

THINKING

CREATIVITY

LATERAL THINKING

ADVERSARY

CONSTRUCTIVE

FORM

CONTENT

I.Q.

OPPORTUNITY SEEKING

PROBLEM SOLVING

CONCEPTS

INFORMATION

DESIGN

ANALYSIS

THE FIRST EARTH BATTALION

19

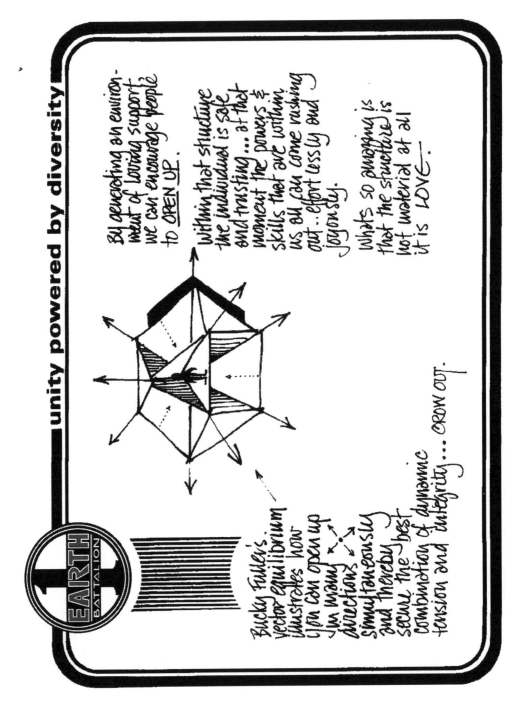

By creating an environment of loving support we can encourage people to OPEN UP.

within that structure the individual is safe and trusting ... at that moment the powers & skills that are within us all can come rushing out .. effort lessly and joyously.

What's so amazing is that the structure is not material at all it is LOVE.

Bucky Fuller's vector equilibrium illustrates how you can open up in many directions simultaneously and thereby secure the best combination of dynamic tension and integrity... GROW OUT.

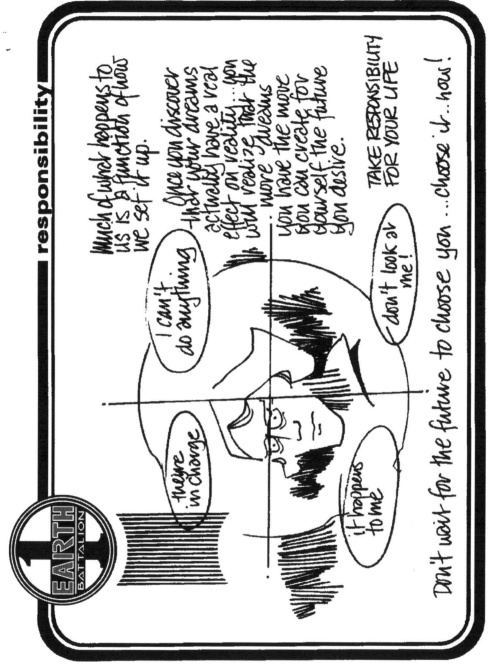

THE FIRST EARTH BATTALION

21

First wave thinkers or flat world folk are apt to raise their index finger and say "I'm gonna tell you one thing!"

The second wave rational or reductionist thinker will assert that this OR that will do... there isn't much middle ground.

The third wave thinker is a possibility thinker. He knows the more options you generate the better your chances to know or succeed at some task. He will say this AND that will do ...according to the situation.

FIRST WAVE

SECOND WAVE

THIRD WAVE

changing your program

its not healthy and its not fun to hold on to ways of thinking that get in the way of our growth. its astonishing how easy it is to give yourself permission to dump programs that don't work. "Cultural cripples" can be healed as fast as they want to be.

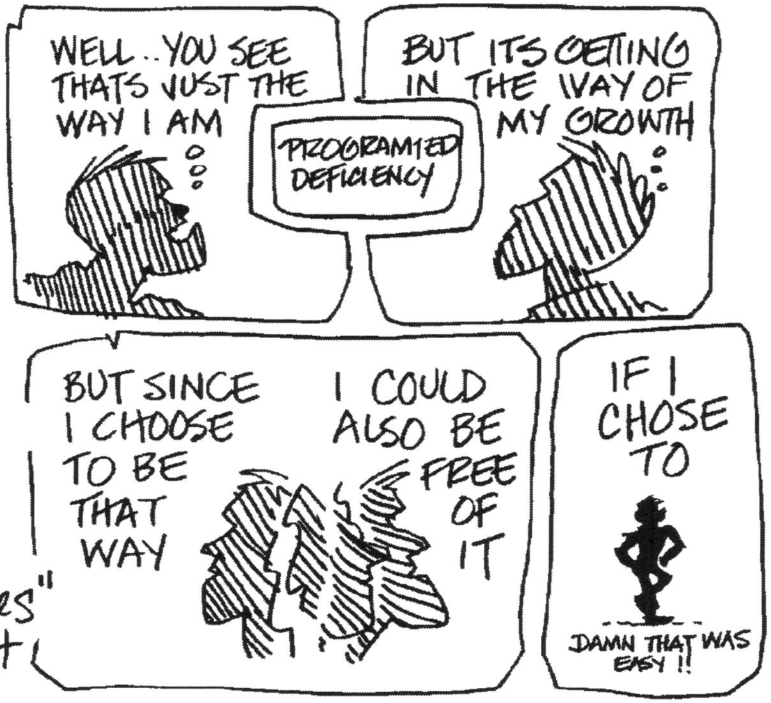
WELL.. YOU SEE THATS JUST THE WAY I AM
PROGRAMED DEFICIENCY
BUT ITS GETTING IN THE WAY OF MY GROWTH
BUT SINCE I CHOOSE TO BE THAT WAY
I COULD ALSO BE FREE OF IT
IF I CHOSE TO
DAMN THAT WAS EASY !!

THE FIRST EARTH BATTALION

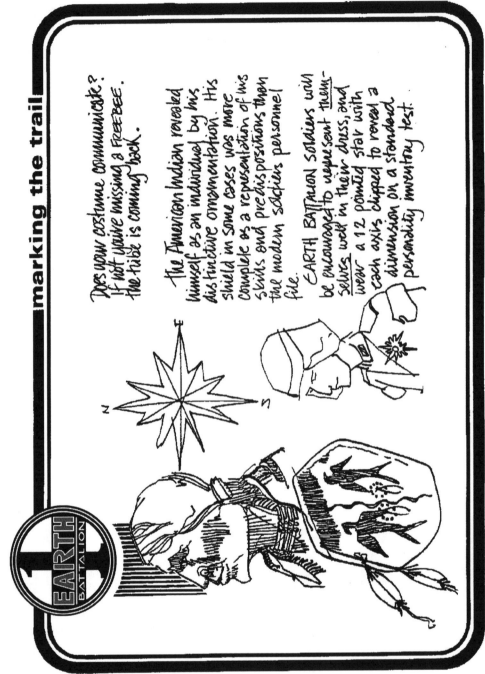

Does your costume communicate? If not you're missing a FREEBEE. The tribe is coming back.

The American Indian revealed himself as an individual by his distinctive ornamentation. His shield in some cases was more complex as a representation of his skills and predispositions than the modern soldiers personnel file.

EARTH BATTALION soldiers will be encouraged to represent themselves well in their dress, and wear a 12 pointed star with each axis chipped to reveal a dimension on a standard personality inventory test.

THE FIRST EARTH BATTALION

One of the most ideal levels of consciousness to be in is attention w/o tension. The attention is a clear and present view of reality. You know intuitively the consequences of everything going on around you but the nice part is that you are centered and grounded in such a way that you can deal with the entire process playing on 45 RPM or maybe even 33⅓ RPM but never 78 RPM.

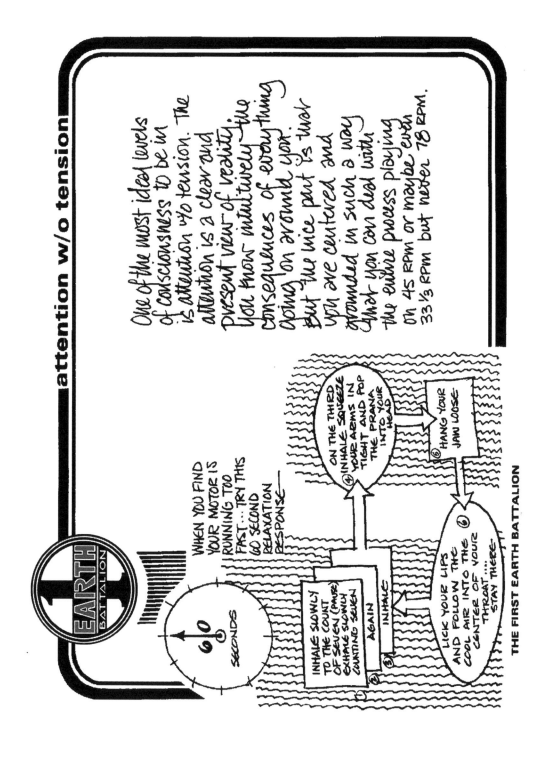

previsualization

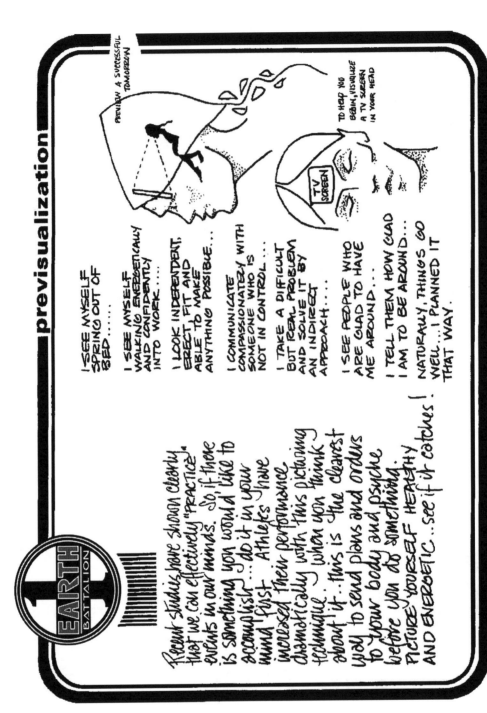

Recent studies have shown clearly that we can effectively "practice" events in our minds. So, if there is something you would like to accomplish...do it in your mind first. Athletes have increased their performance dramatically with this picturing technique... when you think about it...this is the clearest way to send plans and orders to your body and psyche before you do something. PICTURE YOURSELF HEALTHY AND ENERGETIC...see if it catches!

PREVIEW A SUCCESSFUL TOMORROW

I SEE MYSELF SPRING OUT OF BED......

I SEE MYSELF WALKING ENERGETICALLY AND CONFIDENTLY INTO WORK.....

I LOOK INDEPENDENT, ERECT, FIT AND ABLE TO MAKE ANYTHING POSSIBLE...

I COMMUNICATE COMPASSIONATELY WITH SOMEONE WHO IS NOT IN CONTROL...

I TAKE A DIFFICULT BUT REAL PROBLEM AND SOLVE IT BY AN INDIRECT APPROACH.....

I SEE PEOPLE WHO ARE GLAD TO HAVE ME AROUND...

I TELL THEM HOW GLAD I AM TO BE AROUND...

NATURALLY, THINGS GO WELL....I PLANNED IT THAT WAY.

TO HELP YOU BEGIN, VISUALIZE A TV SCREEN IN YOUR HEAD

TV SCREEN

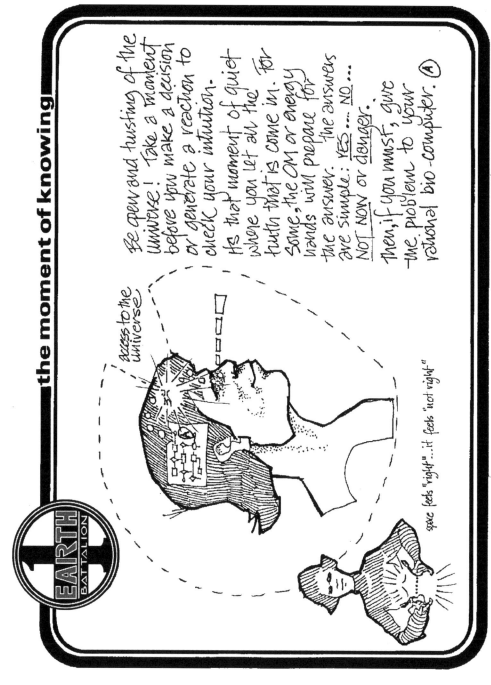

access to the universe

spec feels "right"...it feels "not right"

Be open and trusting of the universe! Take a moment before you make a decision or generate a reaction to check your intuition.

It's that moment of quiet where you let in the truth that is come in. For some, the OM or energy hands will prepare for the answer. The answers are simple: YES ... NO .... NOT NOW or danger.

Then, if you must, give the problem to your rational bio-computer. Ⓐ

omni directional thought

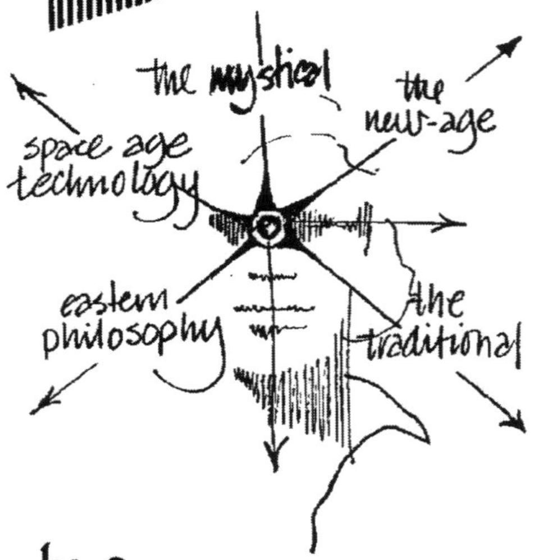

the mystical
the new-age
space age technology
eastern philosophy
the traditional

be a GUERRILLA GURU

Collect strategies by collecting people and points of view. The more you own, the greater your chance of success in any situation.

OMNI-DIRECTIONAL THOUGHT

The first EARTH is not mission oriented it is potential oriented. That means we shall continue to look everywhere to find non-destuctive methods of control.

J.F.C. Fuller, the father of mechanized warfare, was an omni-directional thinker and a member of the world of the mystical.

THE FIRST EARTH BATTALION

GO OUTSIDE ——▷ 🔋

Some people live moment to moment ...they're outside. they can see the world from the outside...they read the music of life from the sheet with the notes printed on it.

Other people live in the moment ...they're inside. They feel the world with their bodies and they live the music of life by grooving on the things and moods that come to them. The conscious warrior stays awake enough to choose the way to process experience to best support the mission of service and enjoy it!!

when working with others or doing "head work" its good to go outside and check on your objectivity. How do you look...is it working?

GO INSIDE! A warrior-monk who must go from point A to point B will shift his consciousness to his one point and REALLY GET INTO WALKING.

5th BELOW NAVEL

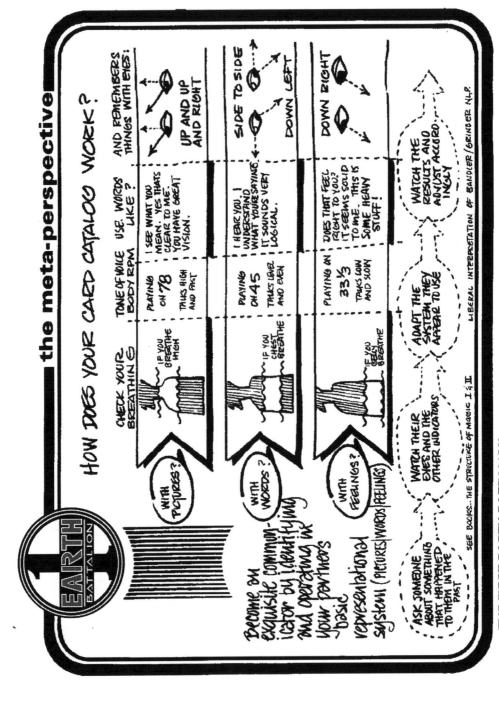

the meta-perspective

HOW DOES YOUR CARD CATALOG WORK?

Become an exquisite communicator by identifying and operating in your partner's basic representational system (PICTURES|WORDS|FEELINGS)

WITH PICTURES?

WITH WORDS?

WITH FEELINGS?

CHECK YOUR BREATHING / IF YOU BREATHE HIGH

IF YOU CHEST BREATHE

IF YOU BELLY BREATHE

TONE OF VOICE BODY RPM
PLAYING ON 78 — TALKS HIGH AND FAST
PLAYING ON 45 — TALKS LEVEL AND EVEN
PLAYING ON 33⅓ — TALKS LOW AND SLOW

USE WORDS LIKE?
I SEE WHAT YOU MEAN. YES THATS CLEAR TO ME. YOU HAVE GREAT VISION.
I HEAR YOU. I UNDERSTAND WHAT YOUR SAYING. IT SOUNDS VERY LOGICAL.
DOES THAT FEEL RIGHT TO YOU? IT SEEMS SOLID TO ME. THIS IS SOME HEAVY STUFF!

AND REMEMBERS THINGS WITH EYES:
UP AND UP AND RIGHT
SIDE TO SIDE — DOWN LEFT
DOWN RIGHT

ASK SOMEONE ABOUT SOMETHING THAT HAPPENED TO THEM IN THE PAST

WATCH THEIR EYES AND THE OTHER INDICATORS

ADAPT THE SYSTEM THEY APPEAR TO USE

WATCH THE RESULTS AND ADJUST ACCORDINGLY

SEE BOOKS... THE STRUCTURE OF MAGIC I & II

LIBERAL INTERPRETATION OF BANDLER / GRINDER NLP

THE FIRST EARTH BATTALION

EARTH BATTALION

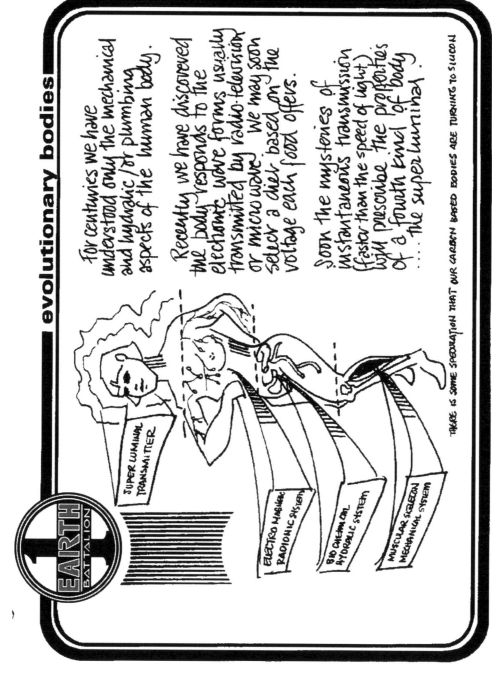

For centuries we have understood only the mechanical and hydraulic /or plumbing aspects of the human body.

Recently we have discovered the body responds to the electronic wave forms usually transmitted by radio·television or microwave. We may soon select a diet based on the voltage each food offers.

Soon the mysteries of instantaneous transmission (faster than the speed of light) will prescribe the properties of a fourth kind of body ....the super luminal.

SUPER LUMINAL TRANSMITTER

ELECTRO MAGNETIC RADIONIC SYSTEM

BIO CHEMICAL HYDRAULIC SYSTEM

MUSCULAR SKELETON MECHANICAL SYSTEM

THERE IS SOME SPECULATION THAT OUR CARBON BASED BODIES ARE TURNING TO SILICON

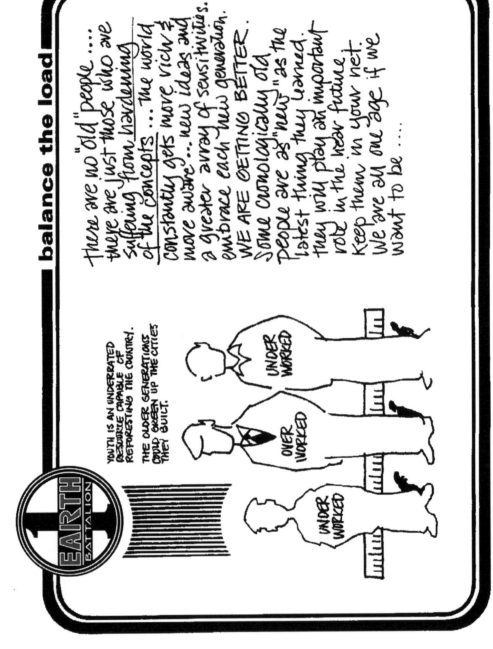

There are no "old" people .... they are just those who are suffering from hardening of the concepts ... the world constantly gets more rich & more aware ... new ideas and a greater array of sensitivities embrace each new generation. WE ARE GETTING BETTER. Some cronologically old people are as "new" as the latest thing they learned. They will play an important role in the near future. Keep them in your net. We are all one age if we want to be .....

YOUTH IS AN UNDERRATED RESOURCE CAPABLE OF REFORESTING THE COUNTRY.

THE OLDER GENERATIONS COULD GREEN UP THE CITIES THEY BUILT.

UNDER WORKED

OVER WORKED

UNDER WORKED

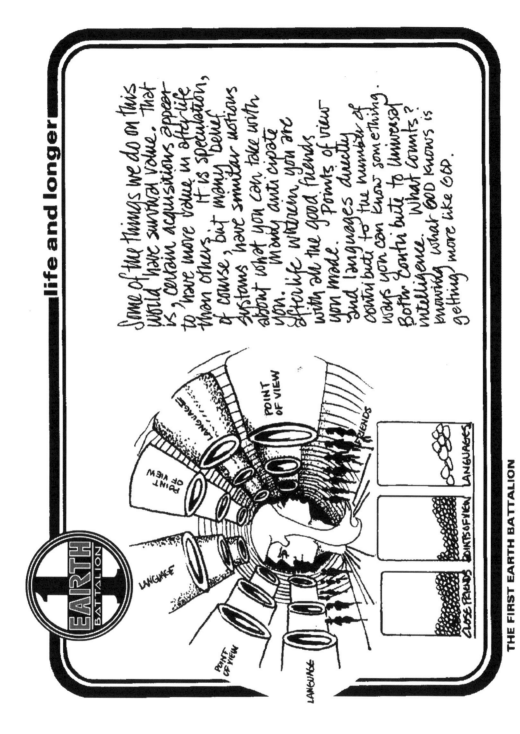

Some of the things we do on this world have survival value. That is, certain acquisitions appear to have more value in after life than others. It is speculation, of course, but many belief systems have similar notions about what you can take with you. Many anticipate after life wherein you are with all the good friends you made. Points of view and languages directly contribute to the number of ways you can know something. Both contribute to universal intelligence. What counts? Knowing what GOD knows is getting more like GOD.

POINT OF VIEW

POINT OF VIEW

LANGUAGE

LANGUAGE

POINT OF VIEW

LANGUAGE

FRIENDS

CLOSE FRIENDS	POINTS OF VIEW	LANGUAGES

THE FIRST EARTH BATTALION

33

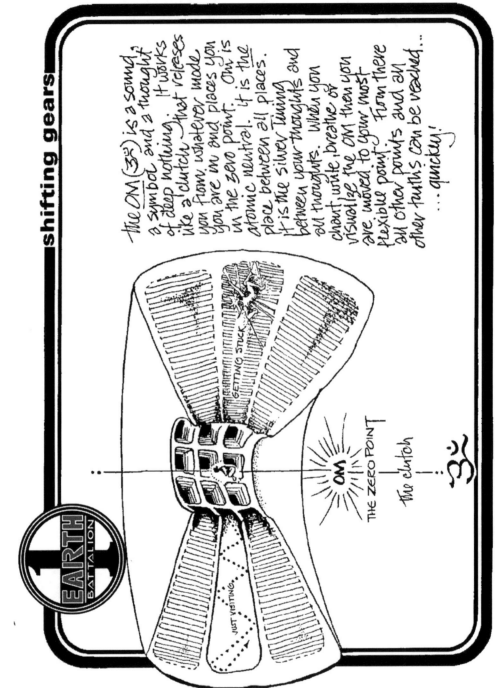

The OM (ॐ) is a sound, a symbol and a thought of deep nothing. It works like a clutch that releases you from whatever mode you are in and places you in the zero point. OM is the atomic neutral. It is the place between all places. It is the silver tuning between your thoughts and all thoughts. When you chant, write, breathe or visualize the OM then you are moved to your most flexible point. From there all other points and all other truths can be reached... quickly!

GETTING STUCK

JUST VISITING

THE ZERO POINT

OM

The clutch

ॐ

One of the grandest moments
in personal development
trainings is to watch people
"pop out of the jelly" caught
out of their lives in a set of
belief systems that have
blocked them from realizing
we are all one family......
often a serving experience
like warfare ...or a truly
loving group of friends that
causes people to realize
they are CONNECTED to all of
those around them in
a deep & profound way.

this is the planets nearest
spectator sport ....
CONSCIOUSNESS WORK

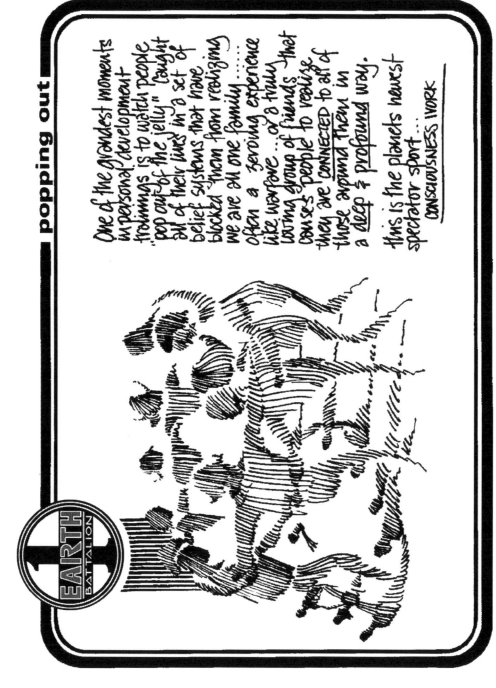

PHASE I. Locate/address/catagorize the community organizations in your region. Have a way to call or communicate with each.

PHASE II. Determine the kinds of service each can perform. Some groups may only be able to meditate on an idea, others may be able to pack up and work on a dam project out of town for a week. Get the catagories clarified.

PHASE III. Use the network to share information of importance to the community.

PHASE IV. Activate grand networks with regional tasks of interest to all. Do this on friday.

Should a serious problem like an earthquake or financial crash effect your region ... this kind of community cohesion would drastically reduce the chaos and generate the structure for recovery.

A NATIONAL OPERATIONS CENTER FOR WORLD NETWORKING AWAITS MAJOR FUNDING

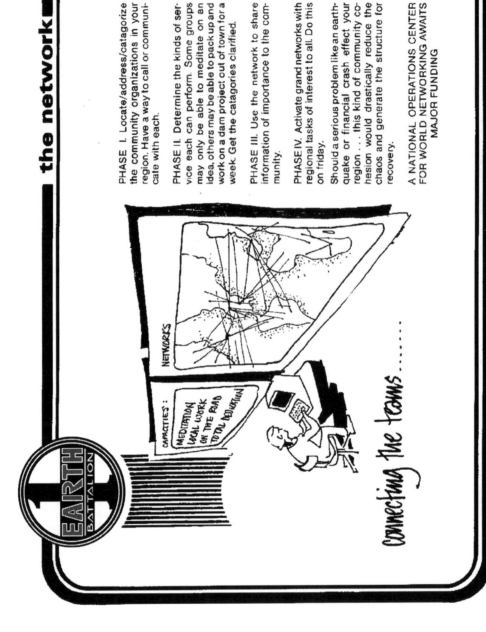

NETWORKS

CAPACITIES:
MEDITATION
LOCAL WORK
ON THE ROAD
TOTAL DEDICATION

connecting the teams........

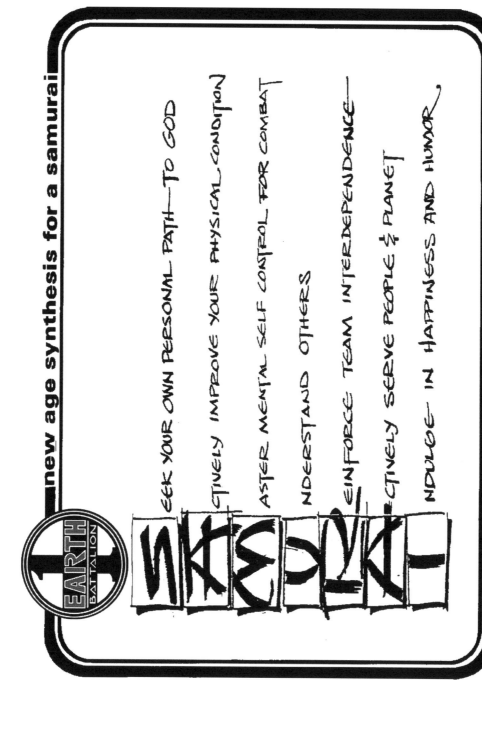

new age synthesis for a samurai

EARTH BATTALION

[S]EEK YOUR OWN PERSONAL PATH — TO GOD

[A]CTIVELY IMPROVE YOUR PHYSICAL CONDITION

[M]ASTER MENTAL SELF CONTROL FOR COMBAT

[U]NDERSTAND OTHERS

[R]EINFORCE TEAM INTERDEPENDENCE —

[A]CTIVELY SERVE PEOPLE & PLANET

[I]NDULGE IN HAPPINESS AND HUMOR,

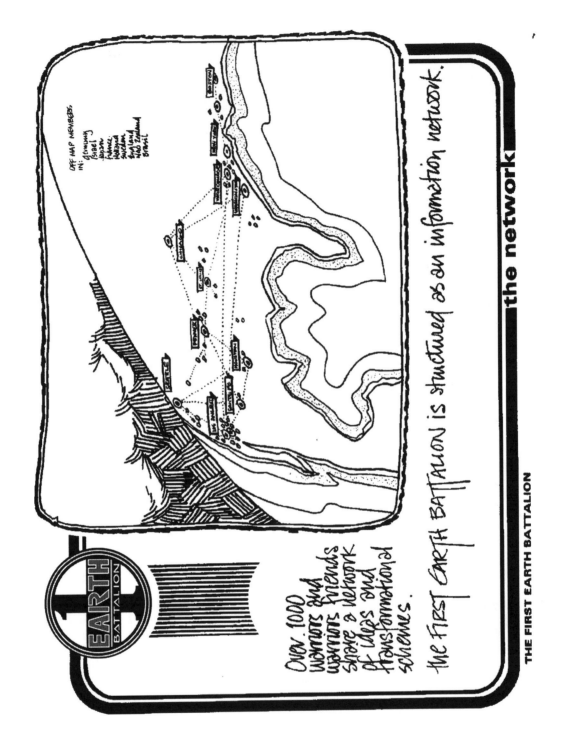

OFF MAP MEMBERS
IN:
Germany
Israel
Japan
Malaysia
Sweden
England
New Zealand
Brazil

Over 1000 warriors and warrior friends share a network of ideas and transformational schemes.

the FIRST EARTH BATTALION is structured as an information network.

the network

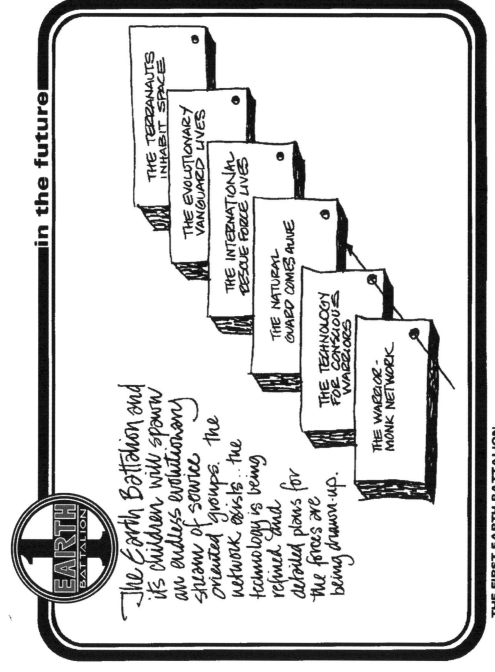

The Earth Battalion and its children will spawn an endless evolutionary spawn of service oriented groups. The network exists... the technology is being refined and detailed plans for the forces are being drawn up.

THE TERRANAUTS INHABIT SPACE

THE EVOLUTIONARY VANGUARD LIVES

THE INTERNATIONAL RESCUE FORCE LIVES

THE NATURAL GUARD COMES ALIVE

THE TECHNOLOGY FOR CONSCIOUS WARRIORS

THE WARRIOR-MONK NETWORK

THE FIRST EARTH BATTALION

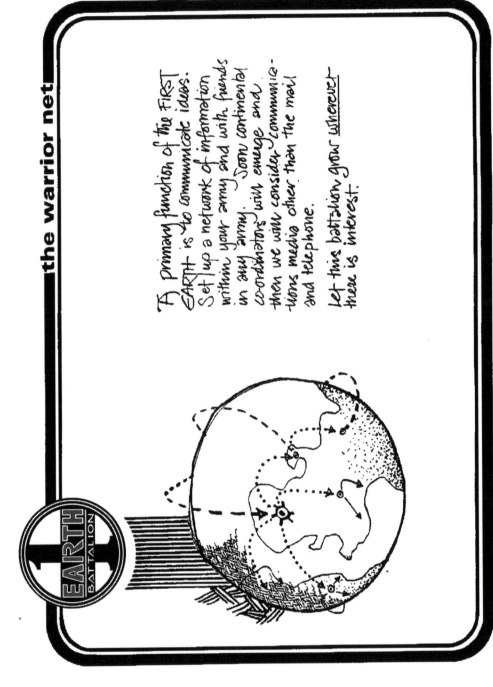

A primary function of the FIRST EARTH is to communicate ideas. Set up a network of information within your army and with friends in any army. Soon continental coordinators will emerge and then we will consider communications media other than the mail and telephone.

Let this battalion grow wherever there is interest.

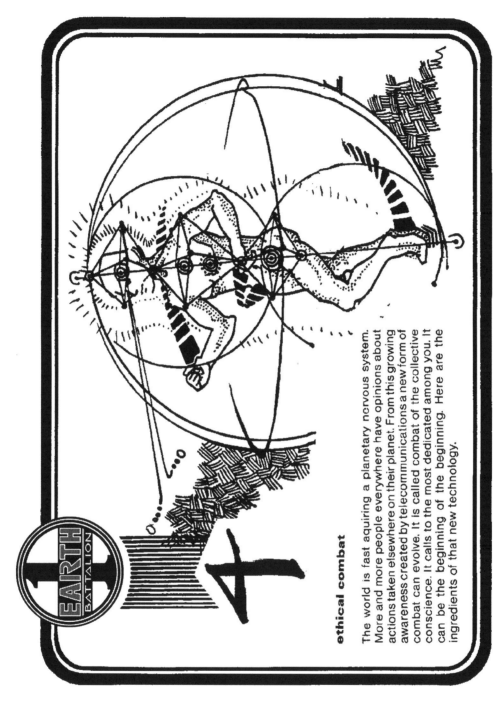

ethical combat

The world is fast aquiring a planetary nervous system. More and more people everywhere have opinions about actions taken elsewhere on their planet. From this growing awareness created by telecommunications a new form of combat can evolve. It is called combat of the collective conscience. It calls to the most dedicated among you. It can be the beginning of the beginning. Here are the ingredients of that new technology.

THE FIRST EARTH BATTALION

ethical combat

Some critical events have occurred that have dramatically shifted the working dynamics of combat. These events and the advance of technical communications combine to create new criteria for winning and losing. Nations and armies that ignore the new ingredients for victory will suffer strange defeats which may grant them the battle but lose them the war.

During a critical moment in the war in Vietnam the world was exposed to the cold-blooded execution of a Viet Cong terrorist by a senior South Vietnamese government official. The news photo and film of this official firing a pistol point-blank into head of the terrorist flashed around the world to an excess of four hundred million people. No explanation could change the visceral and emotional reaction of the world. The South Vietnamese lost that war.

Recently a conflict involving Samoza's regime in Nicaruagua was dramatically changed by an internationally broadcasted killing. A newsman under live camera coverage bellied up to a member of Samoza's army and was shot to death in an apparently non-sensical way. The world watched. Samoza's government fell the next day.

The world with its elaborate international network of interconnected news systems has become a planetary nervous system. Hundreds of millions of people watch the camera-worthy events of any conflict wherein the camera is present. Also, humans all seem to manifest primary gut level reactions to unethical action. Put these elements together and you have established a new style of warfare. We call it the combat of the collective conscience. This combat projects the winning force as one which executes the more ethical action in the face of accompanying cameras. This changes the alternatives to force projection. It portends non-violent combat. It expands the boundaries of action and reaction.

Stategic objectives now include protecting cities. Tactical actions now include the projection of love and concern. The door is opened for joint US and Soviet cooperation.

Words are just one of a number of powerful languages!

If you don't have a language to process a new set of possibilities then you will never know they are there. So, the widest-range of understanding comes to those who have the widest range of language. Those who, likewise have the greatest range of response to a given problem, then have the greatest chance to respond adequately.

THIS TYPE OF LANGUAGE	PROMOTES THIS TYPE OF EFFECTIVENESS
VERBAL (WORDS)	LINEAR, DESCRIPTIVE, ANALYTICAL AND INCREMENTAL COGNITIVE WORK
GRAPHIC (MODELS)	DYNAMIC, INTERDEPENDENT, SYNTHETIC, AND HOLISTIC CONCEPTUAL WORK
CHRONOLOGIC (NET FLOW DIAGRAMS)	SEQUENTIAL, INTERDEPENDENT, TIME BASED, AND COMPLEX EVENTS OR CONSTRUCTION WORK
MATHEMATIC (NUMBERS)	ACCOUNTING, SUPPLY, MONEY, AND OTHER DIGITAL RESOURCE WORK
KINESTHETIC (BODY CONTROLS)	CONSERVATION, STRENGTH, ENERGY, CONTROL AND OTHER ANOLOGIC WORK
CORPORATE (MEETINGS/RITUALS)	SMALL GROUP RELATIONS, COOPERATIVE PLANNING AND OTHER WORK OF COMMITMENT TO PURPOSE
BONDING (DANCING/HUGGING/SINGING)	INDIVIDUAL OPENNESS AND THE DEVELOPMENT OF UNCONDITIONAL LOVE FOR OTHER HUMAN BEINGS.

PEOPLE WHO SCREAM THEY WANT MORE READING/WRITING/& ARITHMATIC DESERVE THE LIMITED WORLD THEY GET WITH THAT LIMITED SET OF LANGUAGES.

THE FIRST EARTH BATTALION

EARTH BATTALION

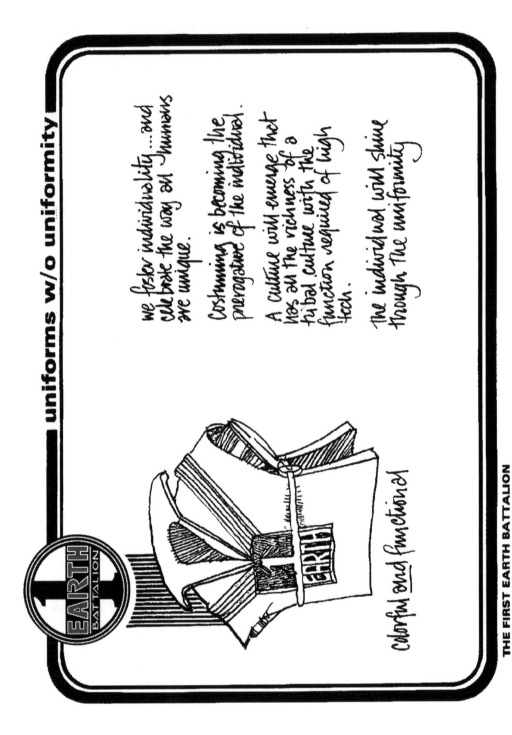

we foster individuality...and celebrate the way all humans are unique.

Costuming is becoming the prerogative of the individual.

A culture will emerge that has all the richness of a tribal culture with the function required of high tech.

The individual will shine through the uniformity

Colorful and _functional_

technology and human potential don't have to be adversary positions... we can use advanced machinery and advanced people.

likewise the idealists on the right and the idealists on the left would do better for all if they worked on the same team.

get comfortable with combining positions and not choosing sides.

this is the third wave way.

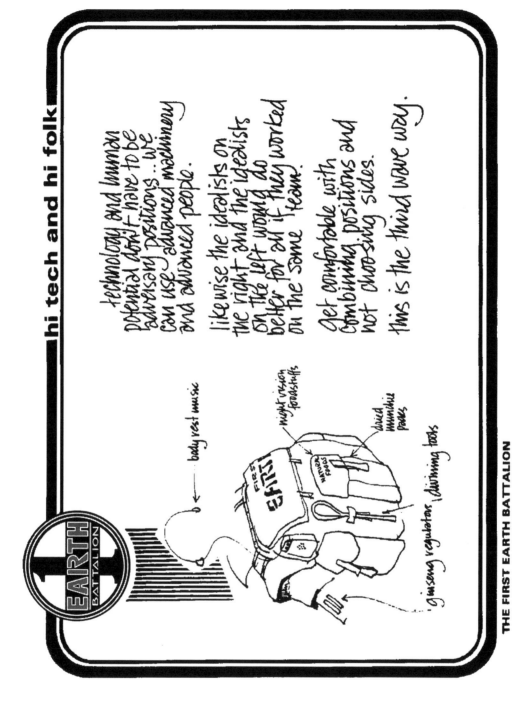

body rest music

night vision food stuffs

dried munchie packs

ginseng regulators / divining tools

THE FIRST EARTH BATTALION

45

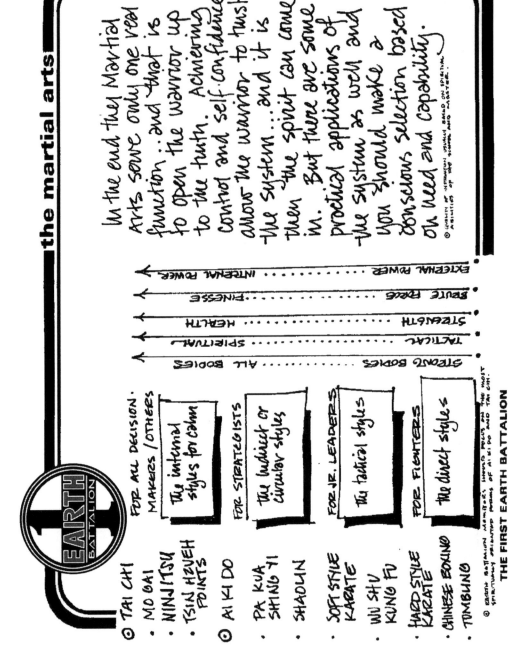

In the end they Martial Arts serve only one real function ... and that is to open the warrior up to the truth. Achieving control and self-confidence about the warrior to trust the system ... and it is then the spirit can come in. But there are some practical applications of the system as well and you should make a conscious selection based on need and capability.

© QUANTITY OF INTENTION USUALLY BASED ON SPIRITUAL ABILITIES OF THE GIVER AND MASTERS.

INTERNAL POWER .... EXTERNAL POWER
FINESSE .... BRUTE FORCE
HEALTH .... STRENGTH
SPIRITUAL .... TACTICAL
ALL BODIES .... STRONG BODIES

FOR ALL DECISION-MAKERS / OTHERS
The internal styles for calm

⊙ TAI CHI
• MO BAI
• NINJITSU
• TSIN HZUEH POINTS

FOR STRATEGISTS
The indirect or circular styles

⊙ AI KI DO
• PA KUA SHING YI
• SHAOLIN

FOR JR. LEADERS
The tactical styles

• SOFT STYLE KARATE
• WU SHU KUNG FU

FOR FIGHTERS
The direct styles

• HARD STYLE KARATE
• CHINESE BOXING
• TUMBLING

© EARTH BATTALION MEMBERS SHOULD FOCUS ON THE MOST SPIRITUALLY ORIENTED FORMS OF AI KI DO AND TAI CHI.

THE FIRST EARTH BATTALION

46

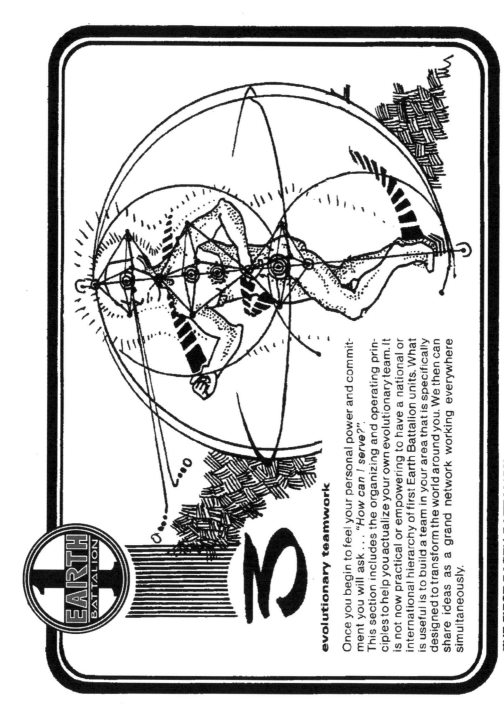

evolutionary teamwork

Once you begin to feel your personal power and commitment you will ask . . . "How can I serve?".
This section includes the organizing and operating principles to help you actualize your own evolutionary team. It is not now practical or empowering to have a national or international hierarchy of first Earth Battalion units. What is useful is to build a team in your area that is specifically designed to transform the world around you. We then can share ideas as a grand network working everywhere simultaneously.

THE FIRST EARTH BATTALION

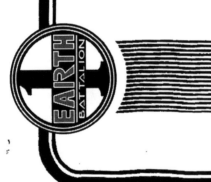

evolutionary teamwork

In recent years there have been some very exciting evolutionary ideas put forward. One confounding factor was that the authors of these ideas were not prepared to organize the enthusiasm generated by their work. The common plea from the readers was ""How can we serve?".

Well, the old rules and models for generating a large organizational structure just didn't seem an appropriate way to harness this new age enthusiasm. One thing that did surface however was that most of the individuals who continuously practiced and were satisfied with evolutionary work were organized in small autonomous groups of close friends. The other organizational development that had power was the network. Since the most powerful resource in the post-industrial world is information . . . the structure that best delivers and organizes information sources is the network.

So, what we are proposing is that if pursuing the Earth Battalion work is exciting to you, then organize your own small group following the suggested steps enclosed. Match the organization to the needs of your community and the personal development needs of your members. Use the First Earth Battalion name, as it empowers your group. When you are organized and operating . . . check back into the network with us and we'll generate some schemes that involve national and international action. Whether you connect into the international network right away is not significant. Think about what level of commitment your team could make when employed for a national concern. Can they leave town? For how many days? To do something physical? We'll let you know about the coordinating developments as they pop.

Use the attached ideas but be creative and enjoy the work and pleasure associated with your own continued growth and enlightened action.

THE FIRST EARTH BATTALION

making time for good work

If we believe in things like peace and taking care of the earth, then we must resource them accordingly. If peace is as important as collecting weapons for national defense, them we must resource peace with the same emphasis.

Since everybody can't insert themselves into an active role in peacemaking every week, we might consider something we can do ... like take care of mother earth. Since the national work force is looking at a four day week, why not make fridays.... EARTH DAY.

On EARTH DAY we spend our time working for PEOPLE AND PLANET. Those of a generation that helped cover the land with concrete ... then begin to cover the concrete with plants ... they can live togther with some design and care. Let the young, who haven't yet begun to worry about environment ... plant one or more trees. These trees can be their investment in a green future. Other larger organizations can replant and refurbish the forests grown up during their lifetimes.

It isn't true that only pure nature can grow the most beautiful habitats. People can consciously design and organize nature in a far superior way. Everyone's neighborhood can be a lush garden with the capability to feed the caretakers in times of need.

That could also be the day that your group met to improve themselves as individuals. A morning of work on the habitat and an afternoon working on self and group.

PEOPLE AND PLANET

THE FIRST EARTH BATTALION

49

Conducting high consciousness commando raids may be confusing to some so here is an example:

CREATING GUERRII LA GURUS . . . .

The most powerful dynamic you can get operating is an independent agent who continues to do transformational work and furthermore generates that same instinct in others. This is called auto-catalytic.

THE CONSPIRACY OF SPARKLING EYES

PHASE 1. Get your team or any large group together. Have them return home and call one or more DJ's in town. Have them report with various kinds of apparent confusion and amazement that "Peoples' eyes are changing . . . somehow beginning to sparkle". They can say that if you stare deeply into someone's eyes near you that you can see an inner light. The IDEA of course is to begin to allow people to appreciate each other's essence by increasing the intensity of eye contact.

PHASE II. The same people call again two weeks later in greater intervals and report: "We have finally discovered how to tell which people got the sparkly eyes first . . . and they can be spotted because they're the ones who automatically hug you upon greeting . . . etc . . . etc.

NOW BE CREATIVE AND GENERATE
SOME MORE OF THE SAME

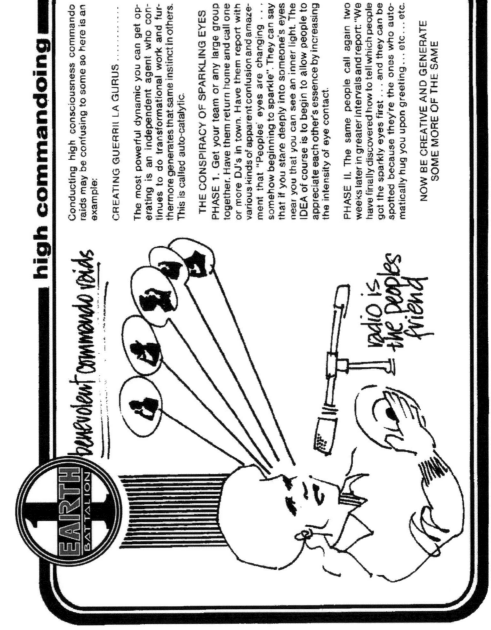

benevolent commando raids

radio is
the Peoples
friend

The FIRST EARTH BATTALION is a grassroots idea. If it doesn't move you to some local team-building action then it isn't ready yet. If it does move you then don't ask to be spoon fed. Put a small team together and begin the WORK.

Mix a program of studying this manual and the related books recommended herein. Discuss things openly and develop a way for the group to pray or otherwise tune in to its higher self. Meet once a week. Begin by working on getting yourself awake, physically smoothed out and eating properly. The rest will follow. Sharing the ways you are improving makes for great group discussion material. Consider the lotus for your own personal program and the arrowed path as the sequence for the group work to follow. Read and discuss the books suggested. Do the trainings suggested if they are convenient to your area.

Once the team feels together and can agree on a benevolent service project, then begin to conduct benevolent raids in order to wake up your community to the truth. We can cooperate with each other, the biosphere and the universe if we choose to.

A circle of harmony is recommended to open and close the meetings. The specific way you do it is unimportant as long as there is a joining of hands and some silence. Right palm over left seems to generate a directional flow within the circle. The process unites the group with each other and the universe. GOOD HUNTING!!

team meeting

① circle of harmony
② sharing indiv. progress
③ alternating reading
④ team plans
⑤ group fun
⑥ closing aspirations

making family

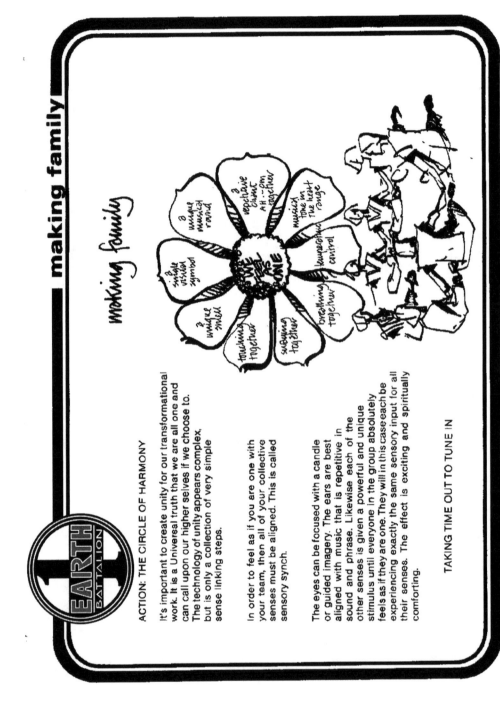

ACTION: THE CIRCLE OF HARMONY

It's important to create unity for our transformational work. It is a Universal truth that we are all one and can call upon our higher selves if we choose to. The technology of unity appears complex, but is only a collection of very simple sense linking steps.

In order to feel as if you are one with your team, then all of your collective senses must be aligned. This is called sensory synch.

The eyes can be focused with a candle or guided imagery. The ears are best aligned with music that is repetitive in sound and phrase. Likewise each of the other senses is given a powerful and unique stimulus until everyone in the group absolutely feels as if they are one. They will in this case each be experiencing exactly the same sensory input for all their senses. The effect is exciting and spiritually comforting.

TAKING TIME OUT TO TUNE IN

THE FIRST EARTH BATTALION

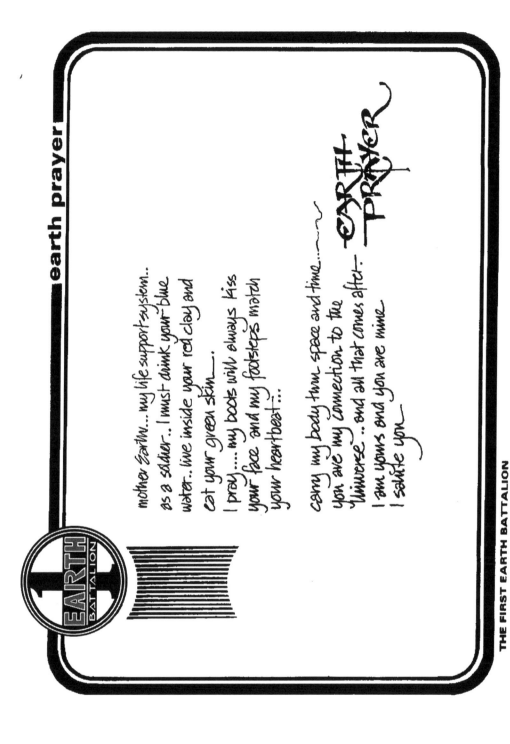

mother earth... my life support system..
as a soldier.. I must drink your blue
water.. live inside your red clay and
eat your green skin...
I pray.... my boots will always kiss
your face and my footsteps match
your heartbeat...

carry my body thru space and time...
you are my connection to the
universe.. and all that comes after..
I am yours and you are mine
I salute you

EARTH
PRAYER

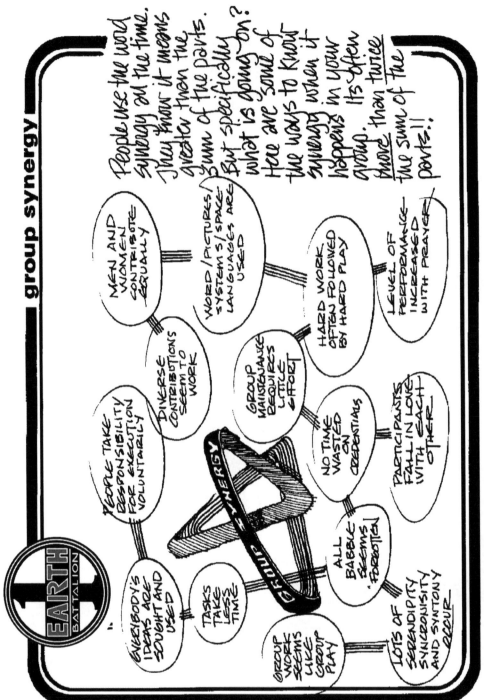

People use the word synergy all the time. They know it means the greater than the sum of the parts. But specifically what is going on? Here are some of the ways to know when it's happening in your group. Its often __more than twice the sum of the parts__!!

MEN AND WOMEN CONTRIBUTE EQUALLY

WORD/PICTURES/SYSTEMS/SPACE LANGUAGES ARE USED

HARD WORK OFTEN FOLLOWED BY HARD PLAY

LEVEL OF PERFORMANCE INCREASED WITH PRAYER

DIVERSE CONTRIBUTIONS SEEM TO WORK

GROUP MAINTENANCE REQUIRES LITTLE EFFORT

PEOPLE TAKE RESPONSIBILITY FOR EXECUTION VOLUNTARILY

NO TIME WASTED ON CREDENTIALS

PARTICIPANTS FALL IN LOVE WITH EACH OTHER

SYNERGY GROUP

ALL BABBLE SEEMS FORGOTTEN

EVERYBODY'S IDEAS ARE SOUGHT AND USED

TASKS TAKE LESS TIME

GROUP WORK SEEMS LIKE GROUP PLAY

LOTS OF SERENDIPITY SYNCHONISITY AND SYNTONY OCCUR

THE FIRST EARTH BATTALION

54

the planetary symbols

identify your team with the other planetary workers!

ACTION: SYMBOL LINKING

There are a set of emerging symbols that can unify all the forces on the planet who are in an evolutionary mode. These windows on the transformational process can more quickly unify global conscious- ness if we can agree to use them whenever and wherever we can.

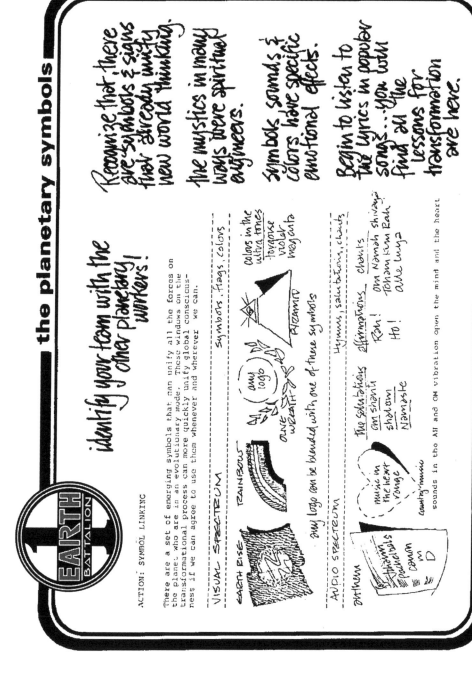

VISUAL SPECTRUM

Symbols, Flags, Colors

EARTH RISE   RAINBOWS

any logo

OUR WREATH

Colors in the ultra tones
turquoise
violet
magenta

PYRAMID

any logo can be blended with one of these symbols

AUDIO SPECTRUM

Hymns, salutations, chants

ANTHEM

music in the heart range

country music

The salutations:
Om shanti
shalom
Namaste

Affirmations
Ra!
Ho!

Chants
Om Namah Shivaya
Tohan Kim Rah
Alle Luya

sounds in the All and OM vibration open the mind and the heart

Recognize that there are symbols & signs that already unify new world thinking.

The mystics in many ways were spiritual engineers.

Symbol sounds & colors have specific emotional effects.

Begin to listen to the lyrics in popular songs... you will find all the lessons for transformation are here.

THE FIRST EARTH BATTALION

55

the curriculum

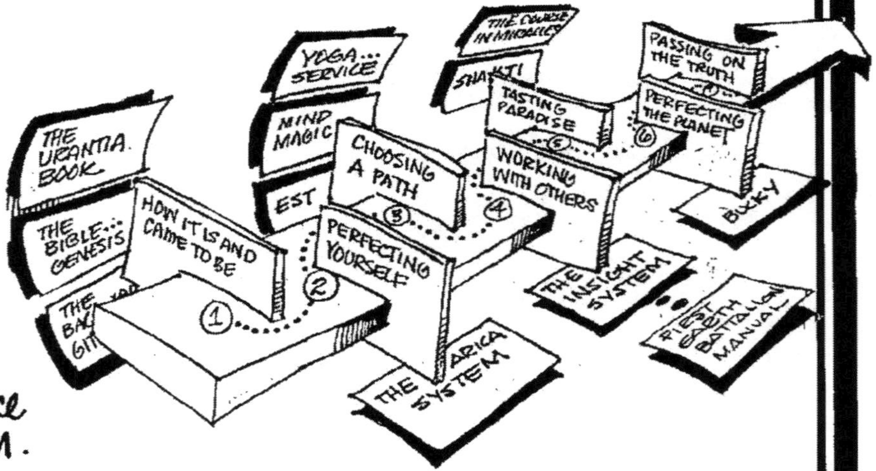
THE URANTIA BOOK
THE BIBLE... GENESIS
HOW IT IS AND CAME TO BE
1
2
YOGA... SERVICE
MIND MAGIC
EST
CHOOSING A PATH
3
PERFECTING YOURSELF
THE ARICA SYSTEM
4
SHAKTI
TASTING PARADISE
5
WORKING WITH OTHERS
THE INSIGHT SYSTEM
6
PASSING ON THE TRUTH
PERFECTING THE PLANET
BUCKY
FIRST EARTH BATTALION MANUAL

this is a possible sequence of actions for any team.

Its just not important that we all do the same things. every team will be unique. Once you get together you will understand this even better. enjoy this adventure!

warriorwork

realization

BODYWORK — The moments when serenity guides your physical conflicts with another or your movement through life.

BIOWORK — The moment when the care of your body instrument is more important than the taste of the food in front of you.

HEADWORK — The moment you begin to see when you are just reacting from a mind program within a culturally induced trance.

HEARTWORK — The moment when you recognize that deep inside we are all one.

SPIRITWORK — The moment that you appreciate the perfect order in the universe, the biosphere and your mind. Then you will sense the power of a masterplan.

PSIWORK — The moment you feel the universe send its own kind of energy tingling through your body and your mind takes off.

ECOWORK — The moment that you know that the plants around you are conscious as well as the air and earth mother below.

PEACEWORK — The moment you dedicate your life to actions on behalf of PEOPLE AND PLANET . . . *then* you have become a player.

FRAMEWORK — The moment you see you can step out of an organizational pattern and reprogram the system.

How will you know when you get there?

Answer these states of being honestly.

and you will be there . . .

THE FIRST EARTH BATTALION

work	objective	reason	color
Bodywork	For physical control/power	To eliminate fear	Dark green
Bodywork	For stamina and control	To shun poison	Light green
Headwork	For flexible behavior	To be free of structure	Yellow
Heartwork	For connections to people	To be free of inferiority	Red
Spiritwork	For connections to spirit	To be free of loneliness	Purple
Psiwork	For connections to universe	To be free of your body	Violet
Ecowork	For connections to the biosphere	To be free of separation	Light blue
Peacework	For connections between people	To be free of tyranny	Dark blue
Framework	For restructuring organizations	To be free of stagnation	Orange

These are the major areas of work for the warrior:

THE FIRST EARTH BATTALION

58

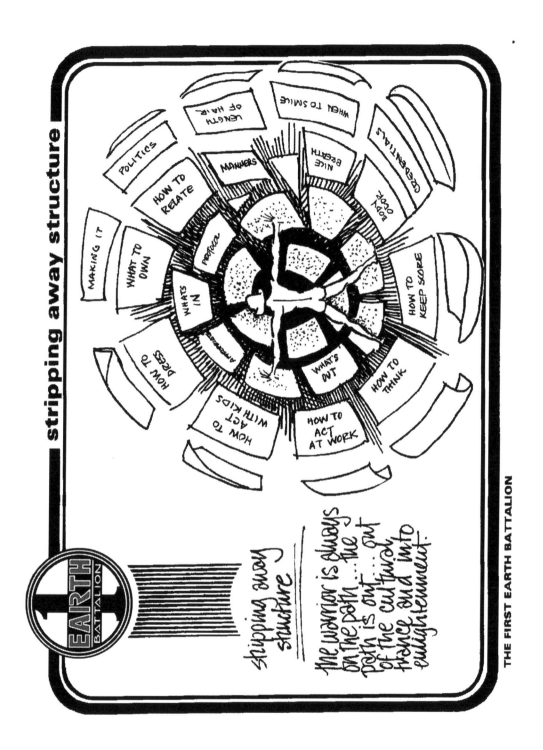

stripping away
structure

the warrior is always
on the path...the
path is out...out
of the cultural
trance and into
enlightenment.

THE FIRST EARTH BATTALION

59

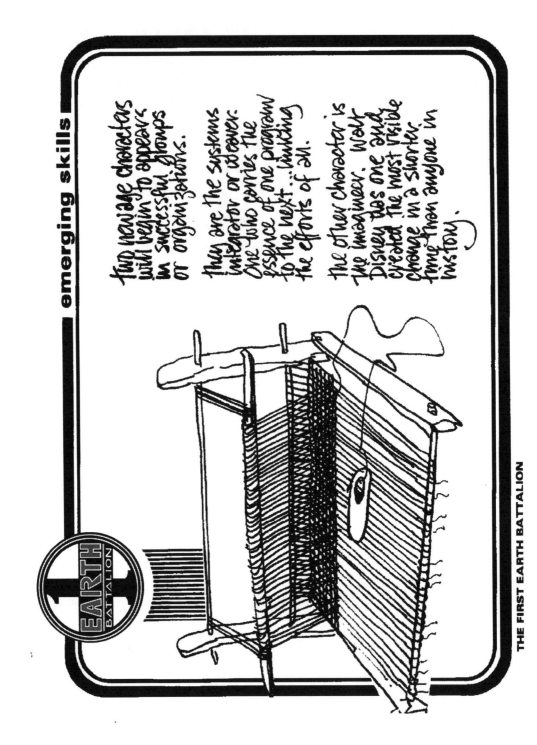

two new age characters will begin to appear in successful groups or organizations.

they are the systems integrator or weaver. One who carries the essence of one program to the next... knitting the efforts of all.

the other character is the imagineer. Walt Disney was one and created the most visible change in a shorter time than anyone in history.

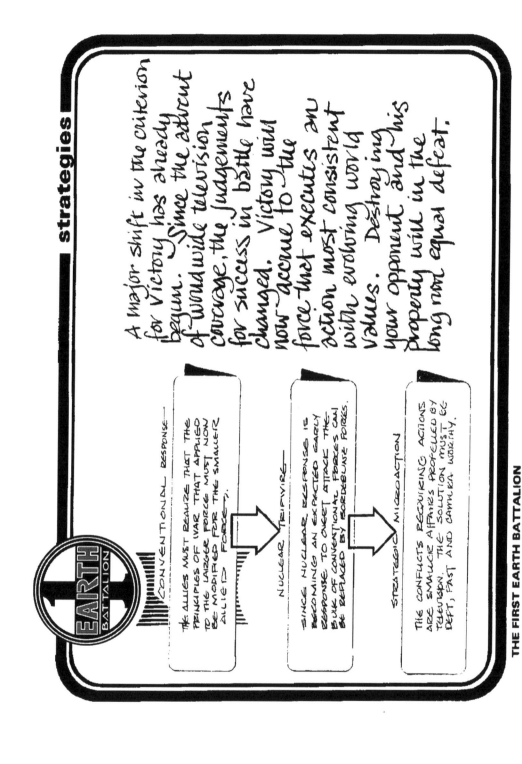

A major shift in the criterion for victory has already begun. Since the advent of worldwide television coverage, the judgements for success in battle have changed. Victory will now accrue to the force that executes an action most consistent with evolving world values. Destroying your opponent and his property will in the long run not equal defeat.

CONVENTIONAL RESPONSE—

THE ALLIES MUST REALIZE THAT THE PRINCIPLES OF WAR THAT APPLIED TO THE LARGER FORCE MUST NOW BE MODIFIED FOR THE SMALLER ALLIED FORCE(S).

NUCLEAR TRIPWIRE—

SINCE NUCLEAR RESPONSE IS BECOMING AN EXPECTED EARLY RESPONSE TO MEET ATTACK THE BULK OF CONVENTIONAL FORCES CAN BE REPLACED BY BORDERLINE FORCES.

STRATEGIC MICROACTION

THE CONFLICTS REQUIRING ACTIONS ARE SMALLER AFFAIRS PROPELLED BY TELEVISION. THE SOLUTION MUST BE DEFT, FAST AND CAMERA WORTHY.

THE FIRST EARTH BATTALION

61

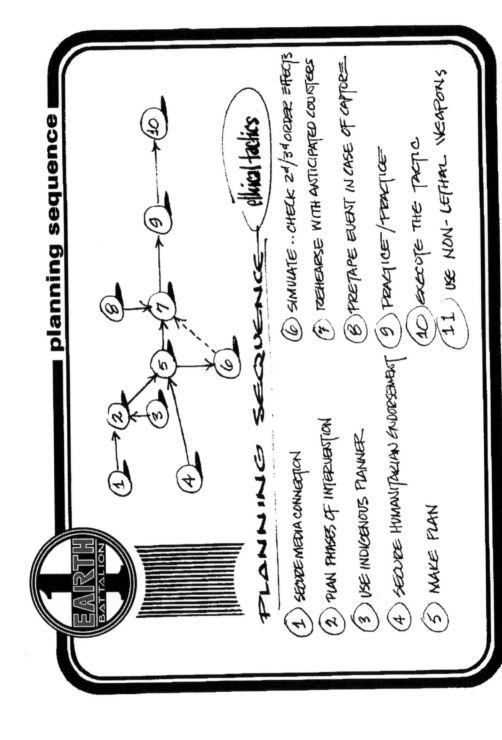

PLANNING SEQUENCE

1. SECURE MEDIA CONNECTION
2. PLAN PHASES OF INTERLUBATION
3. USE INDIGENOUS PLANNER
4. SECURE HUMANITARIAN ENDORSEMENT
5. MAKE PLAN
6. SIMULATE .. CHECK 2d/3d ORDER EFFECTS
7. REHEARSE WITH ANTICIPATED COUNTERS
8. PRETAPE EVENT IN CASE OF CAPTURE
9. PRACTICE / PRACTICE
10. EXECUTE THE TACTIC
11. USE NON-LETHAL WEAPONS

ethical tactics

There are many new kinds of responses to old and emerging world problems ... why not try them?

CONFLICT	NORMAL RESPONSE - BY MILITARY UNIT	SOFT TACTICS RESPONSE	RESPONSIBLE TEAM
HOSTAGES ... iran type situation	high risk	one for one exchange Earth bn w/ hostages	COURAGE FORCE - TM HEART
FANATICS capture of HOLY MONUMENT	high risk	counter demonstration organized by Earth bn.	COUNTER FORCE - TM SPIRIT
AFGHAN type invasion ... communist	little national interest ... no action	unit lines up on border under tension camera	COUNTER FORCE - TM WILL
HOSTAGES ... for mercenary reasons	commando strike (if politically feasible)	same but with world solution	COUNTER FORCE - TM ARMS
ENERGY CRISIS	takes normal conservation steps	builds ecologically solvent community	PIONEER TEAM ECO
URBAN BUDGET with looting chaos	National guard security and crowd control	join university population for solution	PIONEER TEAM URBAN
NOTIFIED OF UNEXPLORED EXTRA TERRESTRIAL LANDING	none planned	set up landing area & language system	PIONEER TEAM SPACE
OIL SPILL IN LOW population both area	not enough military to help!	team begins work to protect biosphere	RESCUE TEAM BIO DISASTER
EARTHQUAKE... FLOOD etc.	National guard assistance	organizes local people into teams	RESCUE TEAM NATURAL DISASTER
HUMAN TRAGEDY... Cambodian genocide	none	organizes popular emergency relief	RESCUE TEAM HUMAN DISASTER

THE FIRST EARTH BATTALION

war has changed

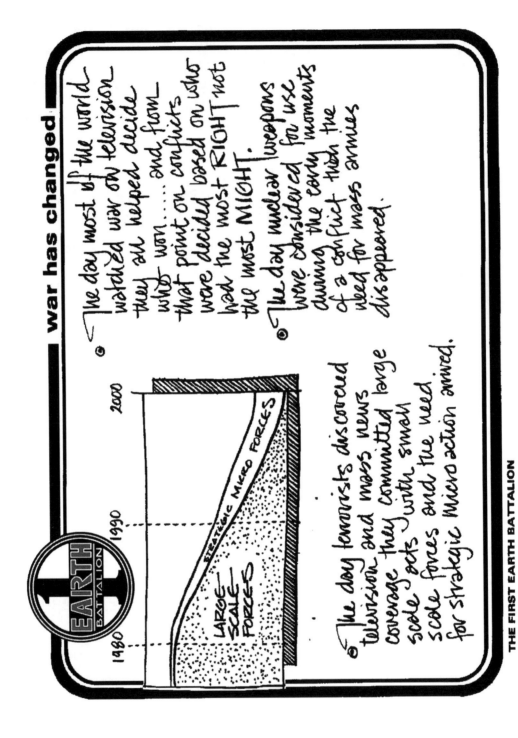

The day most of the world watched war on television they all helped decide who won..... and from that point on conflicts were decided based on who had the most RIGHT not the most MIGHT.

The day nuclear weapons were considered for use during the early moments of a conflict than the need for mass armies disappeared.

The day terrorists discovered television and mass news coverage they committed large scale acts with small scale forces and the need for strategic micro action arrived.

1980   1990   2000

LARGE SCALE FORCES

STRATEGIC MICRO FORCES

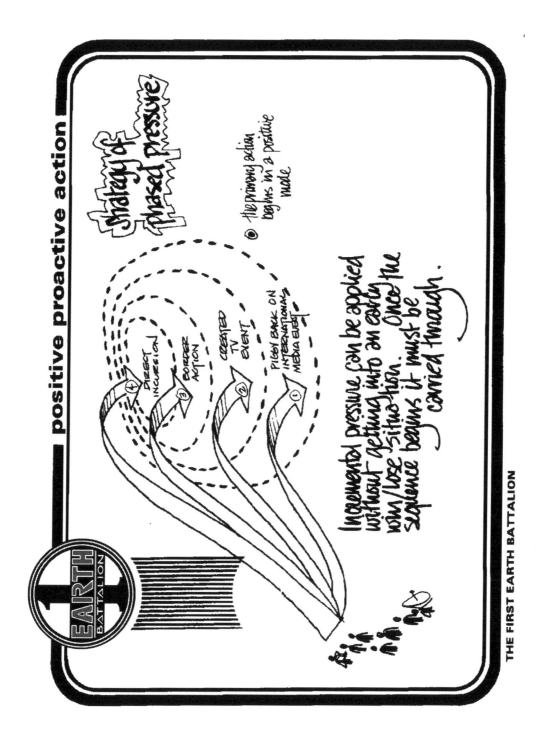

positive proactive action

strategy of
Phased Pressure

⊙ the primary action
begins in a positive
mode

① DIRECT INCURSION
③ BORDER ACTION
② CREATED TV EVENT
① PIGGY BACK ON INTERNATIONAL MEDIA EVENT

Incremental pressure can be applied
without getting into an early
win/lose situation. Once the
sequence begins it must be
carried through.

THE FIRST EARTH BATTALION

65

typical battle scenario
FIRST EARTH

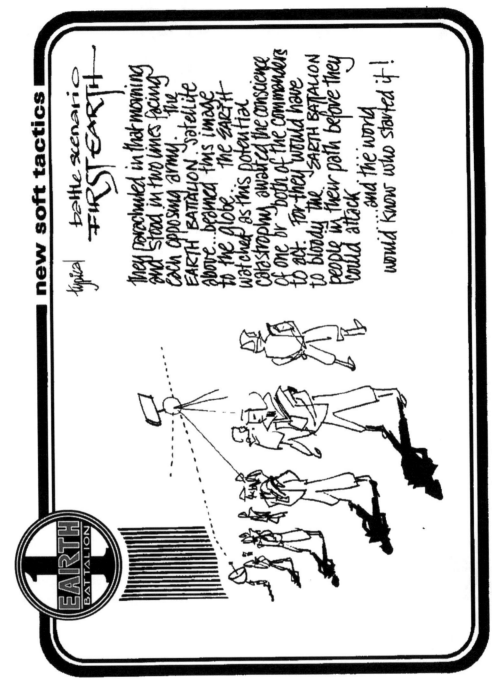

They bivouacked in that morning and stood in two lines facing each opposing army. The EARTH BATTALION satellite above... beamed this image to the globe. The EARTH watched as this potential catastrophy awaited the conscience of one or both of the commanders to act. For they would have to bloody the EARTH BATTALION people in their path before they could attack.

...and the world would know who started it!

THE FIRST EARTH BATTALION

peace technolgy
1 EARTH BATTALION
indigenous music and words of peace
Country flags & spiritual symbols
the battalion carries the symbols and sounds of peace
symbolic flowers
symbolic animal

THE FIRST EARTH BATTALION

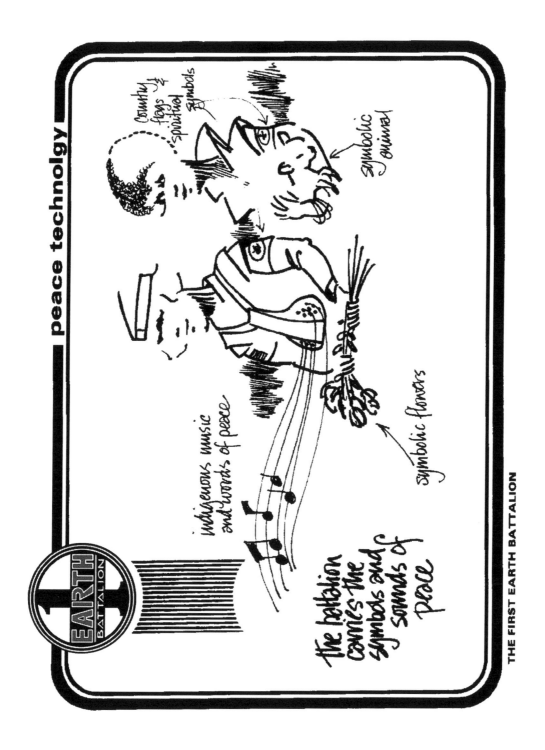

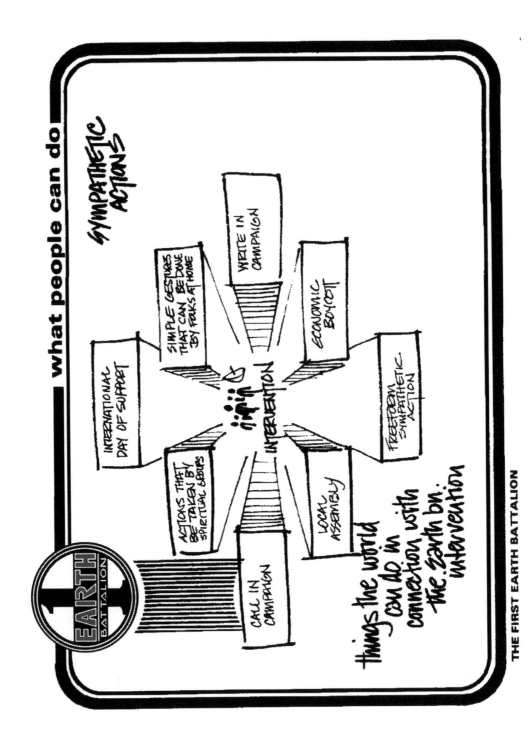

THE FIRST EARTH BATTALION

Warfare currently comprises about 16 dimensions. In 1990 there will be 5 new additions ... or five new areas the tax payers must bear ... or five new possible ways for the ultimate conflict to be triggered.

the five new dimensions are:

- directed energy weapons
- space based platforms
- nuclear terrorism
- changed public awareness
- changed international collective conscience

We need to WORK THESE DIMENSIONS NOW before they begin to work against us!

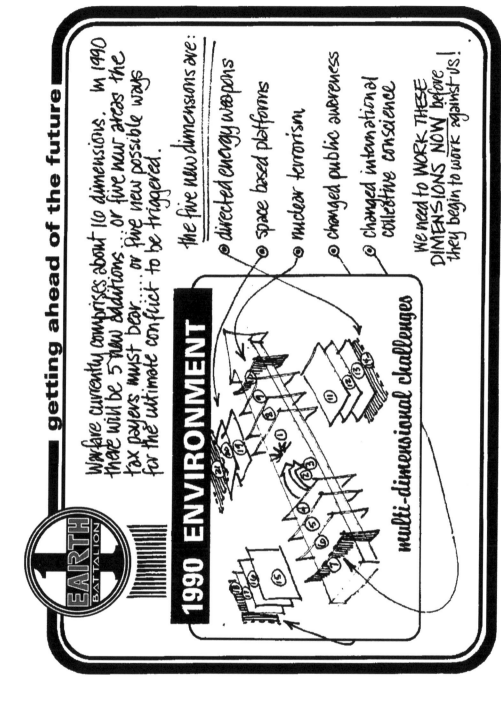

1990 ENVIRONMENT

multi-dimensional challenges

THE FIRST EARTH BATTALION

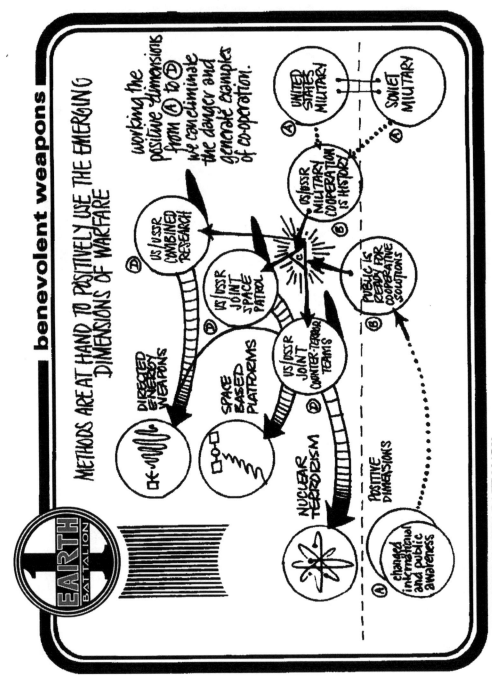

benevolent weapons

METHODS ARE AT HAND TO POSITIVELY USE THE EMERGING DIMENSIONS OF WARFARE

working the positive dimensions from Ⓐ to Ⓓ we can eliminate the danger and generate examples of co-operation.

UNITED STATES MILITARY Ⓐ

SOVIET MILITARY Ⓐ'

US/USSR MILITARY COOPERATION IS HISTORY Ⓑ

US/USSR COMBINED RESEARCH Ⓓ

US/USSR JOINT SPACE PATROL Ⓒ

US/USSR JOINT COUNTER-TERROR TEAMS Ⓓ

PUBLIC IS READY FOR COOPERATIVE SOLUTIONS Ⓑ

DIRECTED ENERGY WEAPONS

SPACE BASED PLATFORMS

NUCLEAR TERRORISM

POSITIVE DIMENSIONS

changed international and public awareness Ⓐ

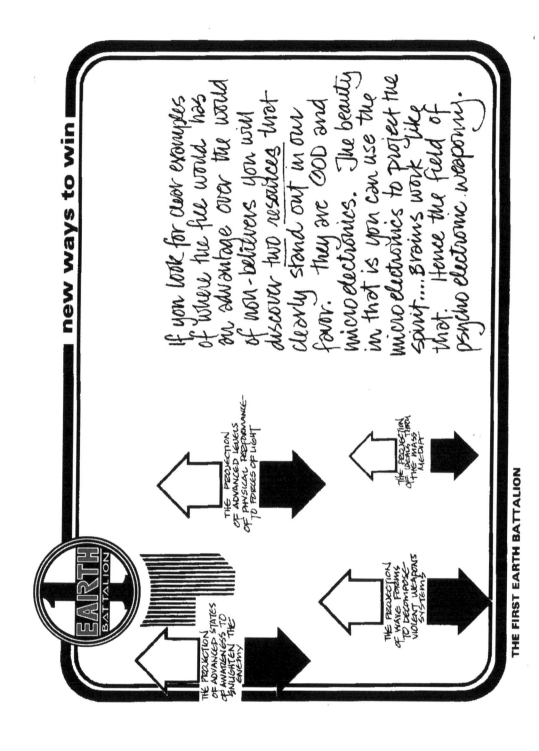

If you look for clear examples
of where the free world has
an advantage over the world
of non-believers you will
discover two resources that
clearly stand out in our
favor. They are GOD and
micro electronics. The beauty
in that is you can use the
micro electronics to project the
spirit....Brains work like
that. Hence the field of
psycho electronic weaponry.

THE PROJECTION
OF ADVANCED LEVELS
OF PHYSICAL PERFORMANCE
TO FORCES OF LIGHT

THE PROJECTION
OF IDEALS THRU
THE MASS MEDIA

THE PROJECTION
OF WAVE FORMS
TO DECOMPOSE
VIOLENT WEAPONS
SYSTEMS

THE PROJECTION
OF ADVANCED STATES
OF AWARENESS TO
ENLIGHTEN THE
ENEMY

EARTH BATTALION

THE FIRST EARTH BATTALION

71

soft combat principles

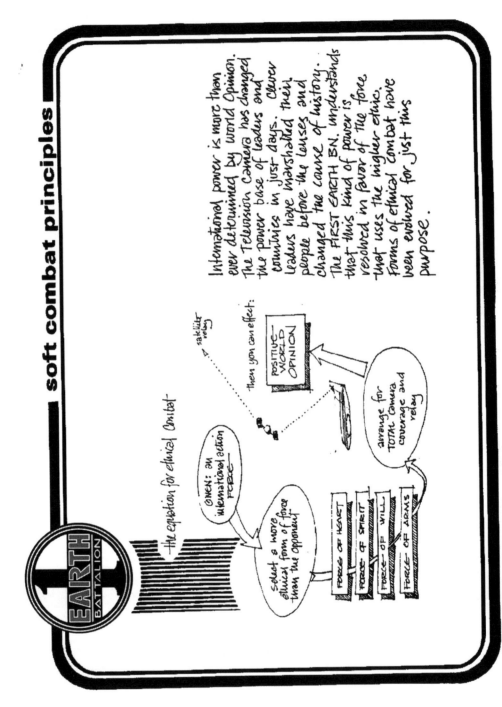

the equation for ethical combat

GIVEN: an international action FORCE

select a more ethical form of force than the opponent

FORCE OF HEART
FORCE OF SPIRIT
FORCE OF WILL
FORCE OF ARMS

arrange for TOTAL camera coverage and relay

then you can effect:
satellite relay

POSITIVE WORLD OPINION

International power is more than ever determined by world Opinion. The Television Camera has changed the power base of leaders and countries in just days. Clever leaders have marshalled their people before the lenses and changed the course of history. The FIRST EARTH BN. understands that this kind of power is resolved in favor of the force that uses the higher ethic. forms of ethical combat have been evolved for just this purpose.

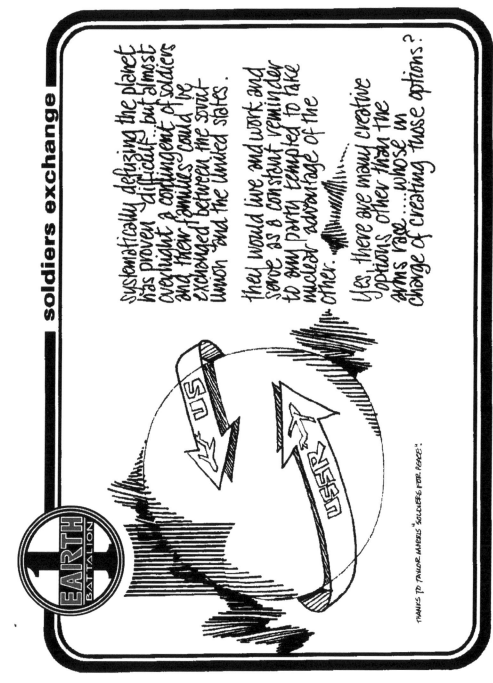

systematically defusing the planet has proven difficult... but almost overnight a contingent of soldiers and their families could be exchanged between the soviet union and the united states.

they would live and work and serve as a constant reminder to any party tempted to take nuclear advantage of the other.

yes, there are many creative options other than the arms race.... whose in charge of creating those options?

THANKS TO TAYLOR HARRIS "SOLDIERS FOR PEACE".

THE FIRST EARTH BATTALION

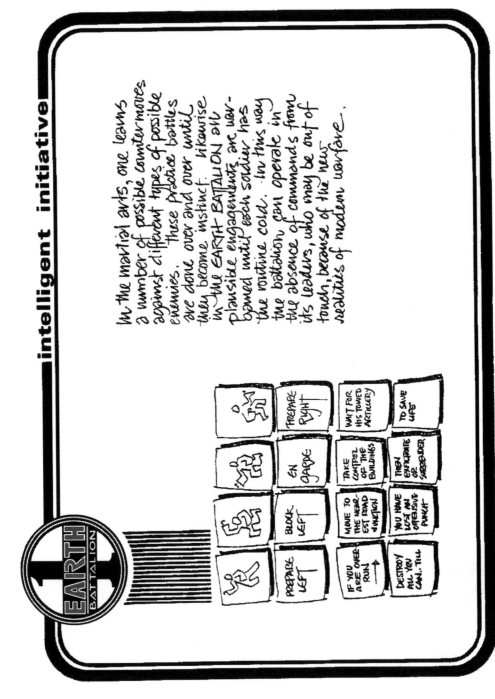

In the martial arts, one learns a number of possible counter-moves against different types of possible enemies. These practice battles are done over and over until they become instinct. Likewise in the EARTH BATTALION all plausible engagements are war-gamed until each soldier has the routine cold. In this way the battalion can operate in the absence of commands from its leaders, who may be out of touch, because of the new realities of modern warfare.

EN GARDE
PREPARE RIGHT
BLOCK LEFT
PREPARE LEFT
TAKE CONTROL OF THE BUILDINGS
THEN EXPLOITATE OR SURRENDER
MOVE TO THE NEAREST ROAD JUNCTION
YOU HAVE LOST AN OFFENSIVE PUNCH
WAIT FOR HIS TOWED ARTILLERY
TO SAVE LIFE
IF YOU ARE OVER RUN
DESTROY ALL YOU CAN, TILL

THE FIRST EARTH BATTALION

74

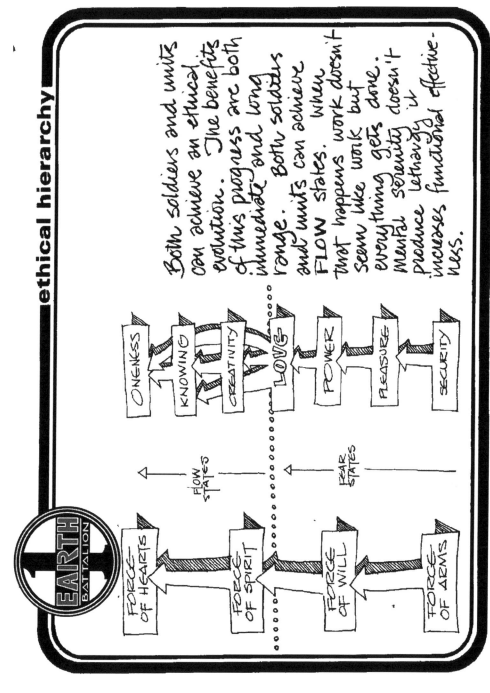

Both soldiers and units can achieve an ethical evolution. The benefits of this progress are both immediate and long range. Both soldiers and units can achieve FLOW states. When that happens work doesn't seem like work but everything gets done. Mental serenity doesn't produce lethargy it increases functional effectiveness.

ONENESS

KNOWING

CREATIVITY

LOVE

POWER

PLEASURE

SECURITY

FLOW STATES

FEAR STATES

FORCE OF HEARTS

FORCE OF SPIRIT

FORCE OF WILL

FORCE OF ARMS

EARTH BATTALION

THE FIRST EARTH BATTALION

75

Martial Arts Principles

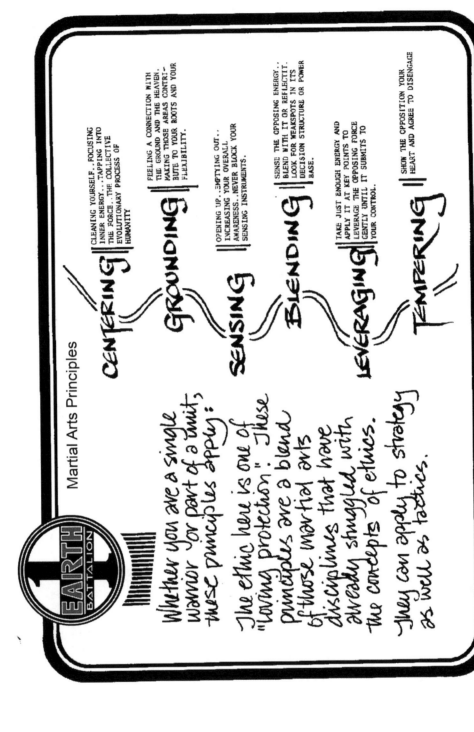

Whether you are a single warrior /or part of a unit, these principles apply:

The ethic here is one of "loving protection." These principles are a blend of those martial arts disciplines that have already struggled with the concepts of ethics.

They can apply to strategy as well as tactics.

CENTERING — CLEANING YOURSELF..FOCUSING INNER ENERGY...TAPPING INTO THE FORCE..THE COLLECTIVE EVOLUTIONARY PROCESS OF HUMANITY

GROUNDING — FEELING A CONNECTION WITH THE GROUND AND THE HEAVEN. MAKING THOSE AREAS CONTRIBUTE TO YOUR ROOTS AND YOUR FLEXIBILITY.

SENSING — OPENING UP..EMPTYING OUT.. INCREASING YOUR OVERALL AWARENESS..NEVER BLOCK YOUR SENSING INSTRUMENTS.

BLENDING — SENSE THE OPPOSING ENERGY.. BLEND WITH IT OR REFLECT IT. LOOK FOR WEAKSPOTS IN ITS DECISION STRUCTURE OR POWER BASE.

LEVERAGING — TAKE JUST ENOUGH ENERGY AND APPLY IT AT KEY POINTS TO LEVERAGE THE OPPOSING FORCE GENTLY UNTIL IT SUBMITS TO YOUR CONTROL.

TEMPERING — SHOW THE OPPOSITION YOUR HEART AND AGREE TO DISENGAGE

THE FIRST EARTH BATTALION

connecting an army of light

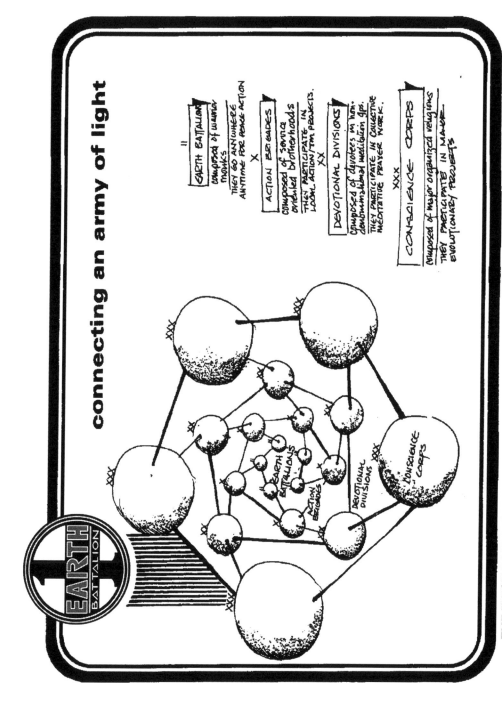

=
EARTH BATTALION
composed of warrior monks
They go anywhere anytime for peace action

X
ACTION BRIGADES
composed of service oriented brotherhoods
They participate in local action/tm projects.

XX
DEVOTIONAL DIVISIONS
composed of devotees in non-denominational meditation gp.
They participate in collective meditative prayer work.

XXX
CONSCIENCE CORPS
composed of major organized religions
They participate in major evolutionary projects

THE FIRST EARTH BATTALION

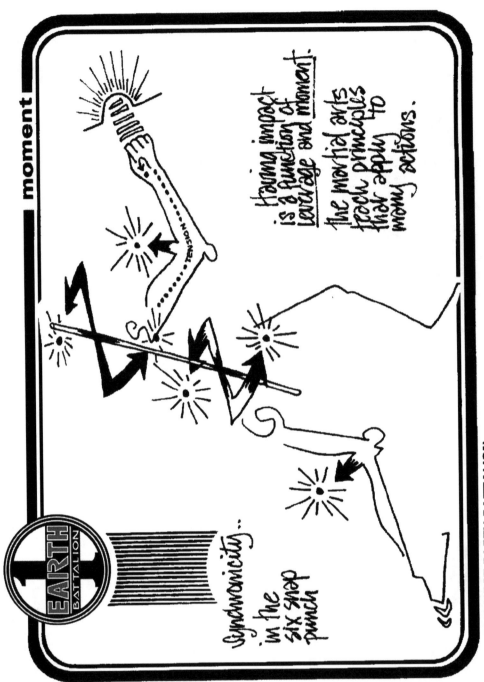

moment

trauma impact is a function of leverage and moment.

the martial arts teach principles that apply to many actions.

Synchronicity... in the six snap punch

x

THE FIRST EARTH BATTALION

78

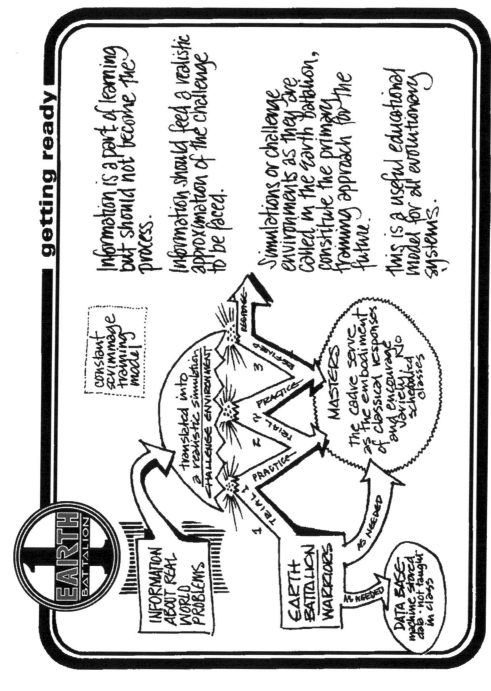

Information is a part of learning but should not become the process.

Information should feed a realistic approximation of the challenge to be faced.

Simulations or challenge environments as they are called in the earth battalion, constitute the primary training approach for the future.

This is a useful educational model for all evolutionary systems.

THE FIRST EARTH BATTALION

79

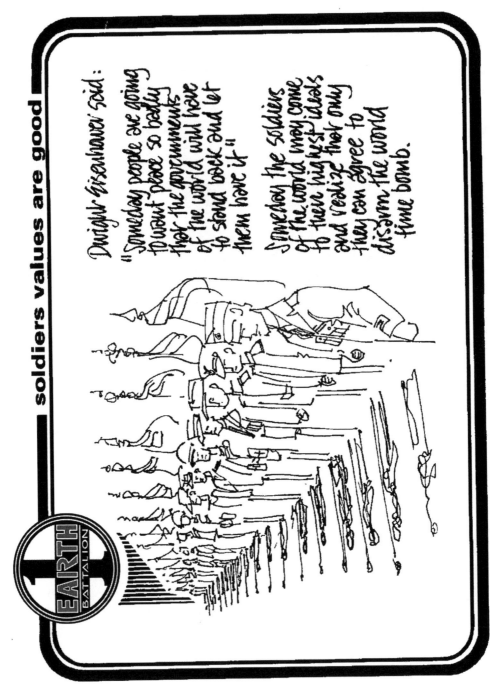

Dwight Eisenhower said:

"Someday people are going to want peace so badly that the governments of the world will have to stand back and let them have it."

Someday the soldiers of the world may come to their highest ideals and realize that only they can agree to disarm the world time bomb.

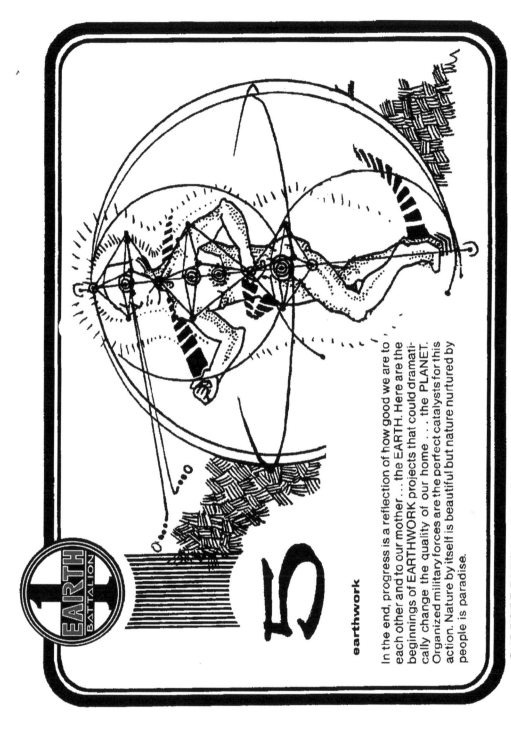

earthwork

In the end, progress is a reflection of how good we are to each other and to our mother . . . the EARTH. Here are the beginnings of EARTHWORK projects that could dramatically change the quality of our home . . . the PLANET. Organized military forces are the perfect catalysts for this action. Nature by itself is beautiful but nature nurtured by people is paradise.

THE FIRST EARTH BATTALION

81

Natural wilderness is wonderful, but can't really compare with the result when man consciously organizes and nurtures the plants and waterways. The lack of care and attention paid to our mother earth is criminal compared with the results that could be forthcoming with a massive organized effort.

Armies have traditionally served as evolutionary agents in organizing and training nature. West Point was established to train military civil engineers. The Corps of Engineers today manages the nation's waterways. The work of massive reforestation for example is a natural for an organization with discipline, communications, and transportation.

Using school children and large elements of the unemployed sector the army could restore the ecological integrity of the earth mother as a primary job. They could support and project large elements of society into the countryside.

When the day comes when a large combat force isn't needed to fight abroad then the alternatives to combat must be surfaced as intelligently thought out plans that can generate the enthusiasm of soldiers and members of the community alike.

Forests can be planted by children propelled to the site by army reserve or active units. These forests could be designed to effect weather patterns, enhance the beauty of the countryside with some interesting planting designs and even be used to make energy efficient pathways for aircraft over the deserts wherein the air is thin. Combining forests with new low energy waterway transportation and new canals would restore the supportive potential of the land to support the nation in an era of diminishing resources.

hark! it's the natural guard

THE FIRST EARTH BATTALION

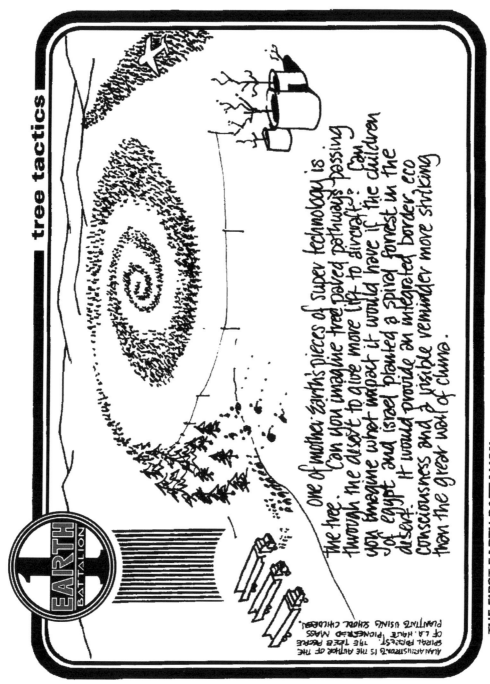

tree tactics

One of mother earth's pieces of super technology is the tree. Can you imagine tree paved pathways passing through the desert to give more lift to aircraft? Can you imagine what impact it would have if the children of egypt and israel planted a spiral forest in the desert. It would provide an integrated border eco consciousness and a visible reminder more striking than the great wall of china.

ALVN ANILLISTRONG IS THE AUTHOR OF THE SPIRAL FOREST. THE TREE PEOPLE OF L.A. HAVE PIONEERED MASS PLANTING USING SCHOOL CHILDREN.

THE FIRST EARTH BATTALION

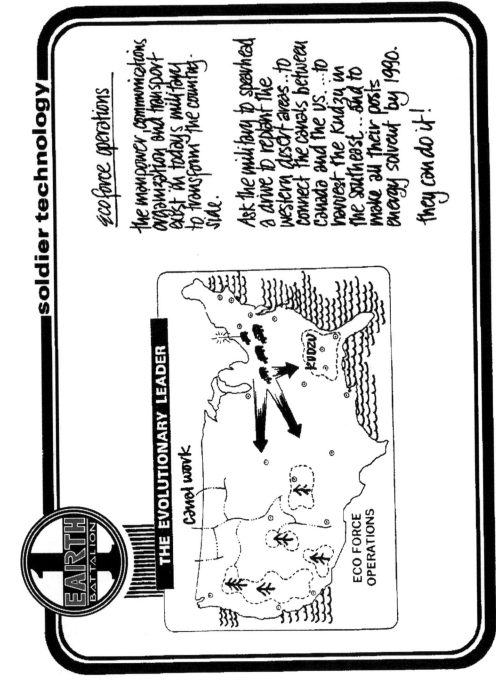

THE EVOLUTIONARY LEADER

Canal work

KUDZU

ECO FORCE
OPERATIONS

ecoforce operations

The manpower, communications, organization and transport exist in today's military to transform the countryside.

Ask the military to spearhead a drive to replant the western desert areas...to connect the canals between Canada and the US...to harvest the kudzu in the southeast...and to make all their posts energy solvent by 1990.

they can do it!

THE FIRST EARTH BATTALION

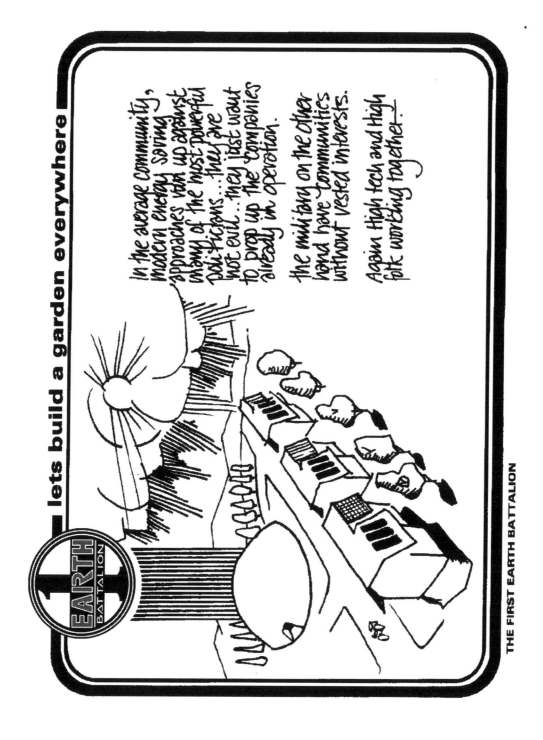

lets build a garden everywhere

In the average community, modern energy saving approaches run up against many of the most powerful politicians...they are not evil...they just want to prop up the companies already in operation.

the military on the other hand have communities without vested interests.

Again high tech and high folk working together.

THE FIRST EARTH BATTALION

85

Military Organizations of the world have all been used to do evolutionary projects.

The American Army has been the leader in evolutionary work in this country:

- race integration
- computer revolution
- advanced schools
- social mobility
- rehabilitation
- sex integration
- systems revolution
- research & development

make them an offer they can't refuse!

an EARTH BATTALION SUGGESTION:

THE ARMY is a key element in the evolutionary jump about to occur. The National Guard will power the ALPHA FORCE in human rescue. The army reserve will catalize major evolutionary projects as the BETA FORCE. The active army will train and run the GAMMA FORCE as they operate strategically to dissolve conflicts. The planning for evolutionary work and the enhancement of paradise is already part of the army's DELTA FORCE.

EARTH BATTALION

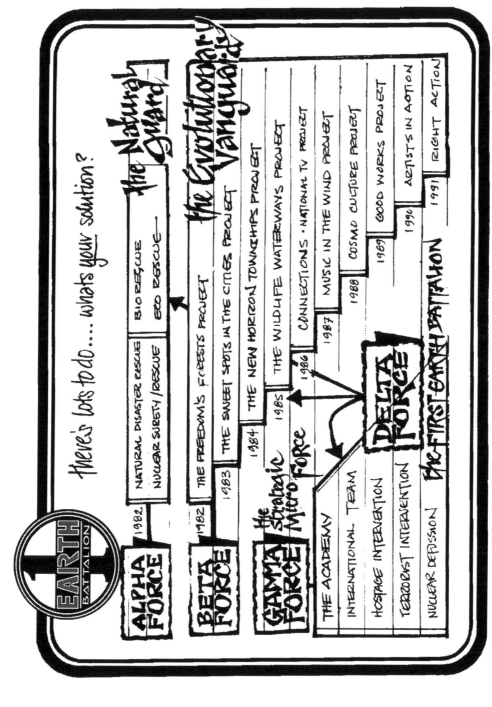

There's lots to do.... what's your solution?

THE FIRST EARTH BATTALION

87

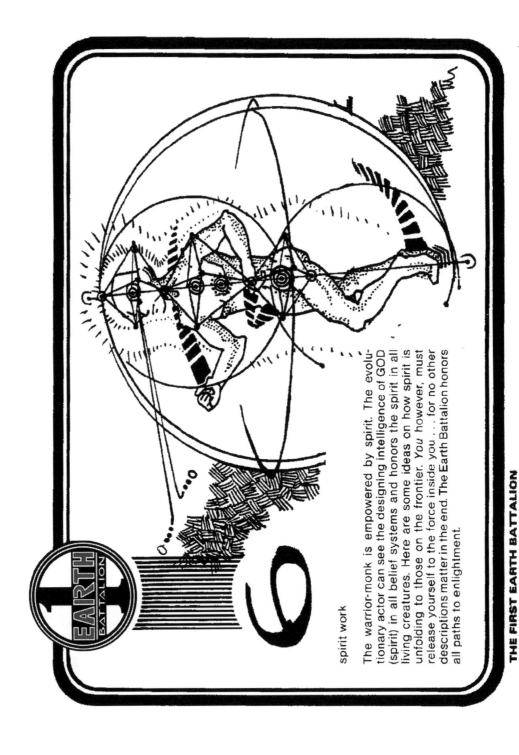

spirit work

The warrior-monk is empowered by spirit. The evolutionary actor can see the designing intelligence of GOD (spirit) in all belief systems and honors the spirit in all living creatures. Here are some ideas on how spirit is unfolding to those on the frontier. *You however, must release yourself to the force inside you . . . for no other descriptions matter in the end.* The Earth Battalion honors all paths to enlightment.

THE FIRST EARTH BATTALION

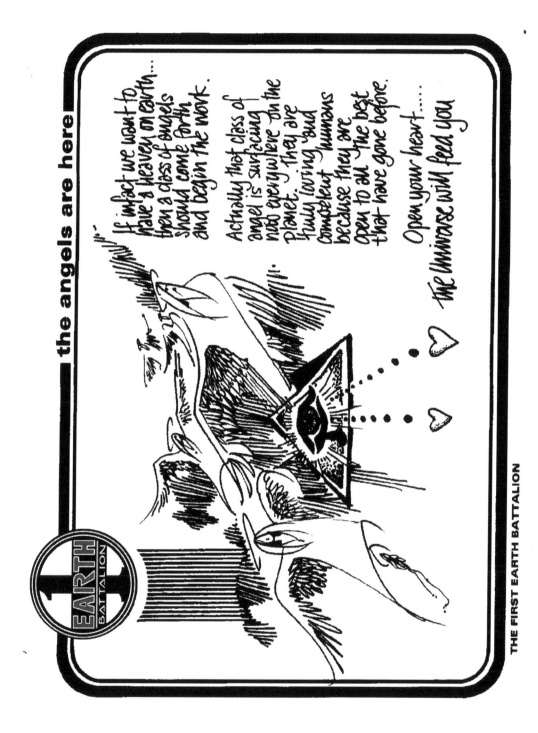

the angels are here

If in fact we want to
have a heaven on earth...
then a class of angels
should come forth
and begin the work.

Actually that class of
angel is surfacing
now everywhere on the
planet. They are
truly loving and
competent humans
because they are
open to all the best
that have gone before.

Open your heart......
the universe will feed you

THE FIRST EARTH BATTALION

89

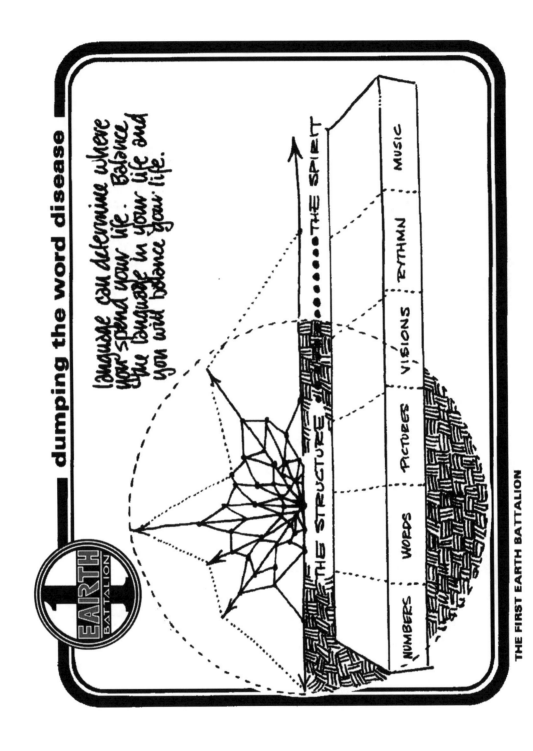

dumping the word disease

language can determine where you spend your life. Balance the language in your life and you will balance your life.

THE SPIRIT

THE STRUCTURE

NUMBERS WORDS PICTURES VISIONS RYTHMN MUSIC

THE FIRST EARTH BATTALION

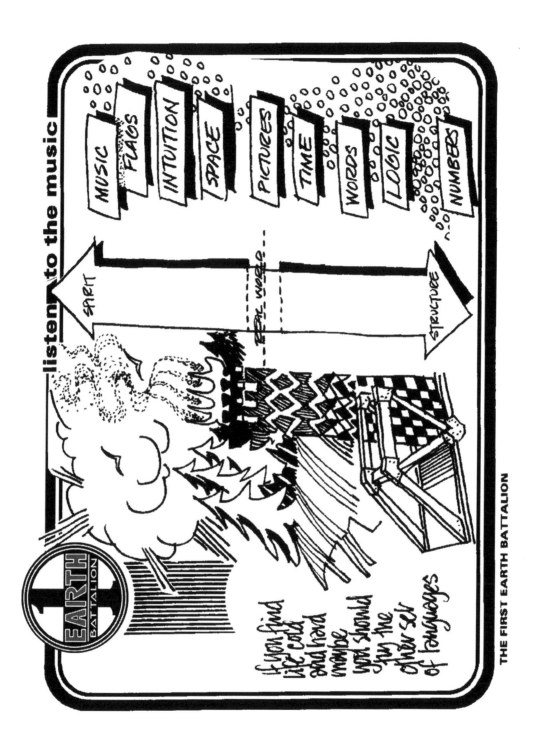

THE FIRST EARTH BATTALION

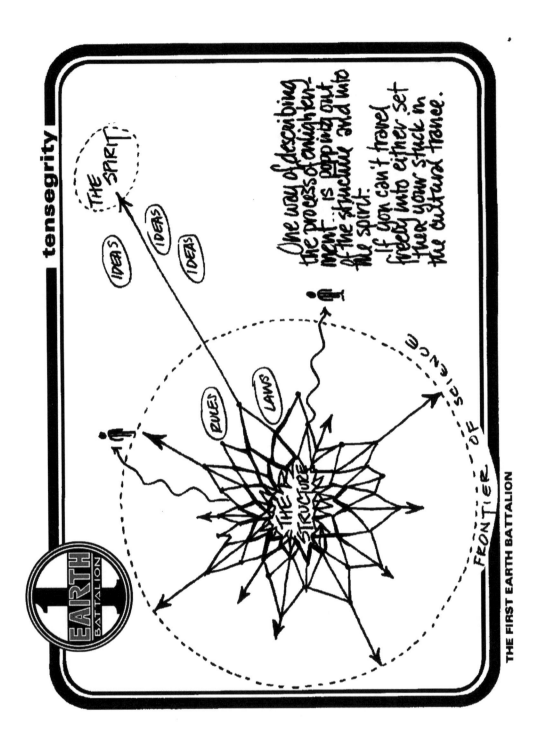

THE SPIRIT

IDEAS

IDEAS

IDEAS

RULES

LAWS

THE STRUCTURE

FRONTIER OF SCIENCE

One way of describing the process of enlighten- ment is popping out of the structure and into the spirit.
If you can't travel freely into either set then your stuck in the cultural frame.

THE FIRST EARTH BATTALION

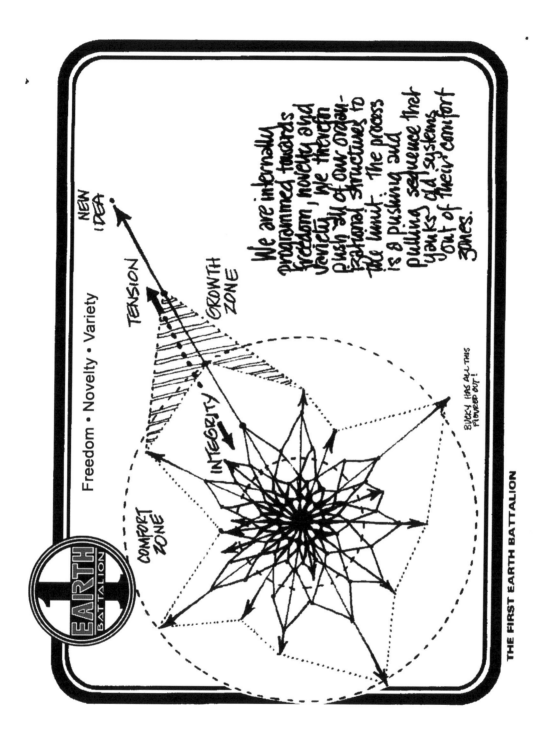

THE FIRST EARTH BATTALION

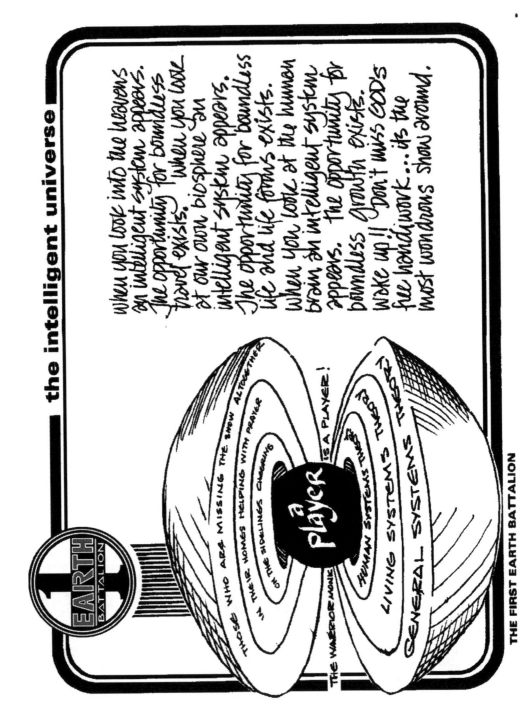

When you look into the heavens an intelligent system appears. The opportunity for boundless travel exists. When you look at our own biosphere an intelligent system appears. The opportunity for boundless life and life forms exists. When you look at the human brain an intelligent system appears. The opportunity for boundless growth exists. Wake up!! Don't miss GOD's fine handiwork... its the most wondrous show around.

EARTH BATTALION

THOSE WHO ARE MISSING THE SHOW ALTOGETHER

IN THEIR HOMES HELPING WITH PRAYER

OR ON THE SIDELINGS CHEERING

a Player

IS A PLAYER!

THE WASHEROREMONIE

HUMAN SYSTEMS THEORY

LIVING SYSTEMS THEORY

GENERAL SYSTEMS THEORY

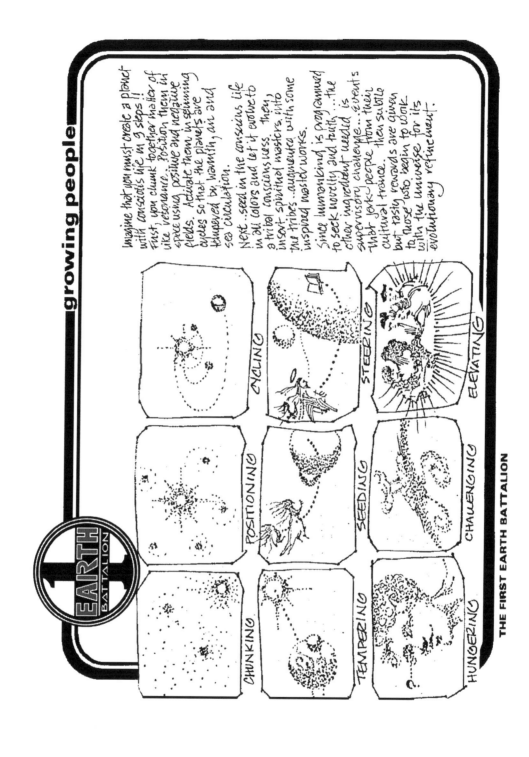

Imagine that you must create a planet with conscious life in 9 steps!!
First, you chunk together matter of like resonance. Position them in space using positive and negative fields. Activate them in spinning cycles so that the planet's are tempered by warmth, air and sea circulation.

Next...seed in the conscious life in all colors and let it evolve to a tribal conscious ness. then, insert spiritual masters into the tribes...augmented with some inspired master works.

Since humankind is programmed to seek novelty and truth...the other ingredient needed is supervisory challenge...events that jerk people from their cultural trance. then subtle but tasty rewards are given to those who begin to work with the universe for its evolutionary refinement.

CYCLING

POSITIONING

CHUNKING

STEERING

SEEDING

TEMPERING

ELEVATING

CHALLENGING

HUNGERING

THE FIRST EARTH BATTALION

95

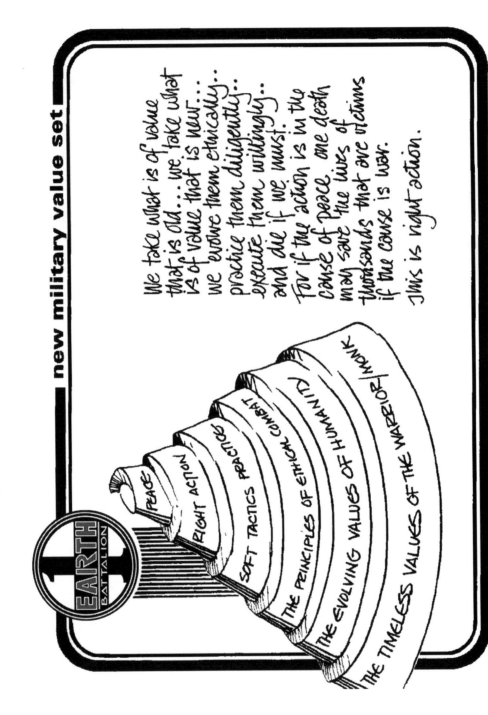

We take what is of value
that is old... we take what
is of value that is new....
we evolve them ethically...
practice them diligently...
execute them willingly...
and die if we must.
For if the action is in the
cause of peace one death
may save the lives of
thousands that are victims
if the course is war.

This is right action.

PEACE

RIGHT ACTION

SOFT TACTICS PRACTICE

THE PRINCIPLES OF ETHICAL COMBAT

THE EVOLVING VALUES OF HUMANITY

THE TIMELESS VALUES OF THE WARRIOR/MONK

THE FIRST EARTH BATTALION

God is _is_ ... and God becomes.

Evolution is what's happening to the universe and therefore evolution is God as a verb.

Evolution is our choice over stagnation or devolution.

Evolution is god's promise to be and to become god. The matter: energy, information and life forms that comprise the is ...are designed in such a way to cooperate with evolution.

We are all ONE @God.
we can be evolution (but you must choose)

THE FIRST EARTH BATTALION

resources

for starters

OUR PAST IS NOT OUR POTENTIAL.

THE AQUARIAN CONSPIRACY by Marilyn Ferguson

| Hardcover edition | $15.00 |
| Softcover edition | 7.95 |

There are many new and exciting resources to assist your team with their personal evolution. Some are written and some are packaged trainings. Depending on whether you have access to a large enough city to do any of the trainings you can choose the written offerings instead. Many of the books must also be purchased in alternative bookstores in relatively large cities. For that reason we have included a larger number of works, many of which should be locally available.

The trainings are all only as effective as the particular trainers you draw. Never-the-less, the trainings we have selected have a national reputation generally worthy of good quality control.

The *URANTIA BOOK* and *COURSE IN MIRACLES* can nicely support weekly discussions. Many of the rest of the books are best used for individual work.

THE FIRST EARTH BATTALION

EARTH BATTALION

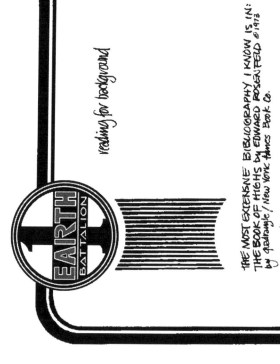

Bibliography

reading for background

THE MOST EXTENSIVE BIBLIOGRAPHY I KNOW IS IN: THE BOOK OF HIGHS by EDWARD ROSENFELD © 1973 by quadragle / NEW YORK times Book Co.

Teilhard de Chardin, Pierre. *The Future of Man.* New York: Harper & Row. 1969.

Teilhard de Chardin, Pierre. *The Phenomenon of Man.* New York: Harper & Row. 1959.

Whorf, Benjamin L. *Language, Thought and Reality.* Cambridge, Mass.: MIT, 1956.

Watts, Alan. *The Book: On the Taboo Against Knowing Who You Are.* New York. Collier, 1966.

Alpert, Richard (Baba Ram Dass) & The Lama Foundation. *Be Here Now.* New York: Crown, 1971.

Castaneda, Carlos. *Journey to Ixtlan.* New York: Simon & Schuster, 1972.

Castaneda, Carlos. *A Separate Reality.* New York: Simon & Schuster, 1971.

Castaneda, Carlos. *The Teachings of Don Juan.* New York: Ballantine, 1968.

Cheng, Man-ching, & Smith, Robert W. *Tai-Chi* Rutland, Vt.. 1966.

DeRopp, Robert S. *The Master Game.* New York: Delta, 1968.

Ehret, Arnold. *A Guide to Rational Fasting.* New York: Lustrum, 1972.

Hall, Edward T. *The Silent Language.* New York: Fawcett, 1959.

Lilly, John C. *Programming and Metaprogramming in the Human Biocomputer: Theory and Experiments.* New York: Julian, 1972.

Lilly, John C. *The Center of the Cyclone.* New York: Julian, 1972.

Masters, Robert E. L., & Houston, Jean. *New Ways of Being.* New York: Viking. In press.

Ouspensky, P. D. *The Fourth Way.* New York: Knopf, 1959.

THE FIRST EARTH BATTALION

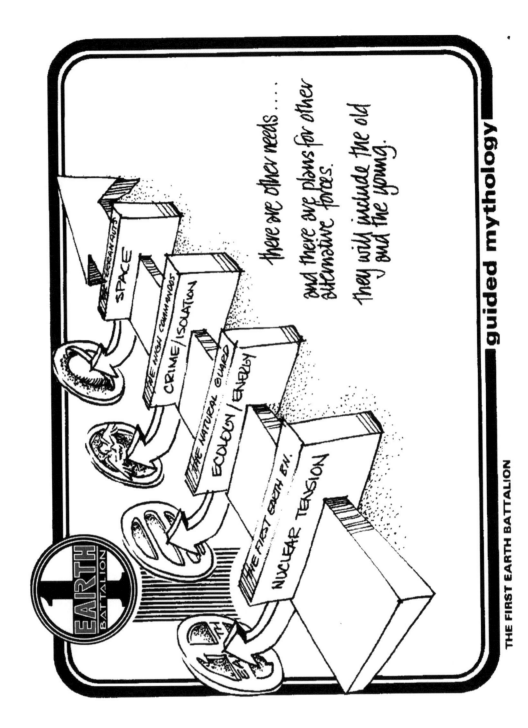

there are other needs....

and there are plans for other alternative forces.

They will include the old and the young.

THE FIRST EARTH BATTALION

100

Home

Thanks friends

SPECIAL THANKS TO:
LISETTE MENCE...LAYOUT
CAROL HOG. PAINTINGS
AN DEES. H.... PROPS
GARY ALLEN.... CONCEPTS
JONATHAN ... MUSIC
CHRISTIAN MARILYN. PAINTING
LOU TICE.... SUPPORT

Jim Channon
LTC. U.S. ARMY

THIS INFORMATION HAS BEEN COLLECTED BY DIRECT EXPERIENCE WITH THE
TRAINERS OR TRAINING MATERIALS CREATED BY OVER 150 NEWAGE GROUPS,
FUTURISTS,PSYCHOTHERAPISTS,THEOLOGIANS,MARTIAL ARTS MASTERS AND A
WIDE ARRAY OF PRACTITIONERS BOTH WESTERN AND EASTERN.ANCIENT AND
MODERN.AND ORTHODOX AND MYSTIC HAVE GENERATED THESE PRACTICAL
RESPONSES TO THE CALL FOR A NEW AGE FOR HUMANKIND. SPECIAL THANKS
IS DUE MARILYN FERGESON,LTC FRANK BURNS,OSCAR ICHASO,COL MIKE
MALONE,BILL HARVEY,LTC JOHN ALEXANDER,BARBARA MARX HUBBARD,LTC
FRANK AKERS,BEA MILLER,JOHN ROGER,OLE NYDAL,GEORGE LEONARD,JOHN
DAVIDSON,BILL HELM,PATRICK WATSON,BOB AND LIA KLAUS,LTC BILL WITT,
SGT D.SHELA REMACK.LTC DENNIS FOLEY,ALAN ARMSTRONG,CAROLYN WYSS,
DR. JERRY EPPLER,COL HOWARD PRINCE,THE DELTA FORCE TEAM,TERRY
DOBSON,THE PACIFIC INSTITUTE,RON MEDVED,THE URANTIA BROTHERHOOD,
MICHAEL NEBADON,GRANT RAMEY,THE CENTER OF THE FORM,NANCY GROSSMAN,
COL TONY POKORNEY,LTG LEE,LAWRIE DERIVORT,BART BOYCE,ALAN GIBB,
JOE MILLER,JOHN MC NEIL,HELEN AND GEORGE BESCH,A HALF A DOZEN
EASTERN GURU'S AND VARIOUS OTHER FOLKS OF QUESTIONABLE ORIGIN.
SPECIAL THANKS TO MY FAMILY RITA,PARKER AND BROOKE WHO FROM TIME
TO TIME PROBABLY QUESTION MY ORIGIN.

EARTH BATTALION

THE FIRST EARTH BATTALION

.....dedication

This mini-course was printed
by HOWARD COMMUNICATIONS.
initial
funds were provided by our
friends at the PACIFIC inst.
special thanks
to SUN BEAR who presented
this work to the great spirit
at the medicine circle
in OJAI.

THE FOUNDATION

Notes:

Made in the USA
Middletown, DE
28 October 2023